And God Created Recovery:

Jewish Wisdom to Help You Break Free From Your Addiction, Heal Your Wounds, and Unleash Your Inner Freedom

Blessings on the journey of recovery!

Rabbi Ilan Glazer

By Rabbi Ilan Glazer

Advance praise for And God Created Recovery....

Rabbi Ilan Glazer has written an important book about Addiction and Recovery. Combining his personal journey with Jewish wisdom and the 12-steps of the Anonymous programs, Ilan has given all of us many insights and paths to Recovery.

As my wife, Harriet Rossetto, founder of Beit T'Shuvah, says: "You don't have to be an addict to be in Recovery." Rabbi Glazer's book is for all of us to find our path to Recovery. Looking at the world today (and in every era) we see the pain and the prejudice that overwhelms us. Rabbi Abraham Joshua Heschel says that prejudice is "an eye disease, a cancer of the soul". Yet, many of us suffer from this eye disease and cancer without realizing it. Rabbi Glazer quotes Thoreau's statement of living "lives of quiet desperation". This is the cancer of the soul and the eye disease!

Rabbi Glazer's book helps all of us remember that the only way to live is in "radical amazement" as Rabbi Heschel teaches. Radical Amazement is the antidote to conventional norms and mental cliches. Reading and living the teachings that Rabbi Glazer presents gives each of us a new pair of glasses, so we may see each day as a new day, filled with wonder and awe.

-Rabbi Mark Borovitz
Senior Rabbi, Beit T'Shuvah

And God Created Recovery is an inspiring resource all rabbis should have on hand to distribute to congregants struggling with addiction. Addiction is on the rise, and we need more voices of healing and hope within the Jewish world. Thanks to Rabbi Glazer for sharing his Torah, and for empowering us all to grow through our suffering and find the healing path we seek. His courage to share his personal story from multiple addictions is an inspiration to me, and I believe it will provide hope to thousands of Jews who read this book.

- Rabbi Laurie Green,
Congregation Bet Mishpachah

Rabbi Glazer courageously takes on a topic that has often been hidden. This book is way overdue. Beyond the everyday challenges that we all face, the Jewish people have been carrying a heavy burden of trauma for more than 2,000 years; addiction occurs when we don't deal with our trauma. May this book help the healing process and help foster deep recovery on all levels.

- Tzadik HaNachash
Founder, Earth Walk and
#Me3Movement

Rabbi Glazer speaks with honesty, urgency, and depth about the tragically taboo subject of addiction in Jewish communities. May his voice lead to a tipping point where stigma gives way to compassion and understanding. Every Jewish educator should read this book.

- Rabbi Derek Rosenbaum
Jewish Text faculty, Charles E. Smith
Jewish Day School

To The Source of All Life, who sustains me,
and enables me to reach this and every day of life,

To my beloved Sherri, who makes every day better,

To my parents, Donna Cilman Glazer and Rabbi Melvin Glazer,
their memories are a blessing,
To my siblings Avi and Debbie, Shoshi, Rafi and Lauren.
and all my loved ones,

To my sponsor, recovery friends,
and all who I've met on the recovery journey,

Thank you.

And to all who still suffer,
may you find healing and wholeness,
in these pages and throughout your lives.

Table of Contents

Rabbi Ilan Glazer

Introduction

"All of life is a challenge of not being distracted
from the greatness that we are."
- Rabbi Yitzhak Kirzner[1]

Addiction takes a terrible toll on the world today. According to the Centers for Disease Control, in 2016, more than 63,600 Americans died from drug overdoses. On average, drug overdoses now kill 174 Americans per day. 16% of state budgets are spent on addiction. Nearly 1/3 of all hospital visits are linked to addiction, and almost half of all emergency room visits for trauma or injury are linked to alcohol. In 2010, 85% of the U.S. prison population were incarcerated for substance related reasons, and more than half of all jail inmates are diagnosed with substance use disorders. The rising costs of addiction exceed $700 Billion annually.[2]

The Jewish community is not immune to the challenges of addiction, though there are very few studies showing the effects of addiction on the Jewish world.

"it appears that a large portion of the North American Jewish community views alcoholism as an illness, has a strong fear of alcoholics, and blames individuals with addictions for their condition. One possible conclusion is that Jewish people believe that members of the Jewish community simply do not become alcoholics, so they are convinced that they are not exposed to people with addictions. Therefore, they lack the ambition to seek education on the topic and become naive to the reality of the prevalence of addictions in the Jewish community... "Over the years, this long legacy of denial among Jews has resulted in unnecessary pain, heartache, and a great deal of alienation from Judaism by those suffering from addiction. It has also served to prevent some suffering Jews from seeking or accepting appropriate help".[3]

A 2014 Israeli study found that 13% of the Israeli population use drugs during their lifetime.[4] A 2015 study of the Winnipeg Jewish community found that of those who responded to the survey, "17.6% stated they have used drugs other than those required by medical reasons, 14.7% of these participants stated that they cannot get through the day without using drugs, and 2.9% reported neglecting their family because of their drug use.... 41.2% reported knowing someone currently struggling with an addiction, and 23.5% of respondents reported having a family history of alcohol or drug abuse."[5] Addiction does not discriminate, and there are thousands of Jews suffering the disease of addiction, yet also thousands of Jews who've found a new life through the principles of recovery. I know this because they are my friends, my teachers, and my guides, and I am in recovery, just like them.

My hope with this book is to give you practical tools and Jewish wisdom to help you through your recovery journey. I'll share stories of my journey, and what I do today to make sure that I stay on a recovery path. Regardless of which particular addiction you or your loved one are faced with; this book can be a powerful part of your healing. For too long, the Jewish community has refused to adequately address the challenge of addiction. A shikr is a goy – only non-Jews are drunks, we've told ourselves. Jews don't have these kinds of problems. Except that of course we do.

Thankfully the Jewish world is starting to realize that we need to be part of the solution, and we need to meet the needs of our people who are struggling to live well. There are a handful of Jewish recovery organizations now, and we must be grateful to Beit T'Shuvah, JACS, Rabbi Dr. Twerski, and others who've blazed a trail. We need many more teachers, many more healers, so that all Jews impacted by recovery can find the healing they seek. No one should have to suffer in silence, and our tradition, like all faith traditions, can and must be part of the answer. This book aims to blend the best of Jewish tradition with the principles of recovery, to show that recovery is kosher, and everyone would benefit from it. I know, however, that every story of recovery is different and what works for me may not work for you. Take what you like and leave the rest. My experience is my own. Yours is just as valid, just as important, just as holy.

A Note on Anonymity

It is a hallmark of recovery behavior that we don't advertise our addictions or our recovery publicly. We work a program of recovery and keep our heads down, lest we be seen as an expert in recovery, or official spokespersons for the fellowships we are a part of. Too many addicts have been attention seeking and spend too much time trying to fix others instead of addressing their own issues.

I am obviously departing from this tradition of total anonymity, and I do so for a few specific reasons. Most importantly, I have benefitted from other recovery works and everyone who has done so has been willing to share their story publicly in order to benefit their readers. I believe that there are people who will be helped with this book and by my willingness to be one voice for healing and recovery. I also know that there are embarrassingly few addiction resources within the Jewish community. There are only a few Jewish rehabilitation centers, and a handful of books, some of which are hard to find, and some of which I don't resonate with. Over the years of my recovery, I wondered why there weren't more Jews talking about recovery. Why are there so few recovery meetings held in synagogues or at Jewish conferences? Why is there no online Jewish recovery community and coaching program? Why aren't we willing to see Jewish wisdom as part of the answer to our recovery needs? My hope is that this book will be the beginning of a movement that helps anyone who needs recovery to find it under Jewish auspices, and I invite you to join me in building that movement. I'll have more to say about that later on.

When we don't talk about addiction, those who struggle with addiction feel as if they can't be fully present, as if only parts of themselves are welcome in Jewish settings. Addicts do have special needs, and the Jewish world all too often has buried its head in the sand, refusing to even admit that addiction is a Jewish issue. We can do better. We must do better. I'm sharing my story in the hope that it will be helpful to those who read it.

I won't be sharing other stories I've heard in recovery rooms – they are not mine to tell, and I honor the spirit of confidentiality agreed to at each meeting. I also am not sharing which fellowships I am a part of, lest anyone think I speak for those fellowships, which I don't. I am leaving out the names of some people whose story has overlapped with my own, and the stories I do share are drawn from experience but have each been altered to maintain anonymity. I have thought long and hard about what to include and what to leave out. I don't want anything I write to cause harm to anyone else. This book is not meant to attack anyone else, and the people who have impacted me negatively have been some of my biggest teachers on my journey. I am grateful to them all and wish them well. I hope you can also be grateful for your teachers, even the ones who were the most difficult to learn from.

Part one of this book provides a foundation for understanding what addiction is, how addicts can recover, a sample of Jewish teachings about addiction and recovery, and highlights of my own recovery journey. In part two, I look at each of the 12 steps from a Jewish perspective, with questions and suggestions for how to enhance your own recovery journey. Part 3 gives you additional perspectives and wisdom that have benefited me on my own journey, and in part four, I invite you to join me in continuing to build a movement of Jewish recovery. Recovery is often isolating, and transformation is hard. This is the kind of book I wanted to read as I was going through the steps and working my program. I hope it is helpful to yours and that together, we can create a movement of healing. Our stories of recovery and healing are precious, yours no less than mine. I believe that all faith traditions can be helpful to their members. Now is a time for us all to step up to the plate and help those who still suffer.

I recognize that not everyone in recovery goes to meetings, not everyone works the steps, and not everyone believes in God. This book will provide you with wisdom that enhances your recovery journey, regardless of which fellowship you are a part of, how far along you are in your recovery, what your level of Jewish practice is, and whether you believe in God. Every journey is unique, and I honor wherever you are in your recovery. I'm grateful to my atheist and non-Jewish recovery friends I've met in the fellowships. I've learned so much from them, as well as my Jewish friends. Please feel free to adjust the exercises I offer to suit your own recovery needs. Write your own prayers and affirmations. Sing your own songs. As always, take what you like and leave the rest. If something doesn't speak to you, feel free to adapt it, skip it, or come back to it another time. Please note that many of the texts I quote assume a male reader and a male God. In my own personal practice, I use different names for God, and thinking of God as only masculine doesn't work for me. God contains all genders, all emotions, and all of life. While I honor the texts and left them in as they are, please feel free to use whatever God-language works for you.

I do want to emphasize that I do not speak for any recovery fellowship. I am also not a medical provider. I am a rabbi, a storyteller, a spiritual director, a musician, a podcast host, and a transformation coach. This book is a journey for the soul, with practical steps to grow through the dark nights of the soul and find healing, serenity, and wholeness on the other side. I cannot guarantee any specific transformation that will occur in your life from following what I outline in this book. That said, a Chinese proverb states that "if we don't change our direction, we're likely to end up where we're headed." This book invites you to examine your life, to see how addiction has impacted your story, to write new chapters of healing, and to step into the beautiful world that I know is possible for each and every one of us.

This journey of transformation is hard work. My teacher Rabbi Zalman Schachter-Shalomi taught that "changing your life is like changing a flat tire while still driving the car". This journey requires us to be brave, authentic, vulnerable, and courageous. Thankfully, we don't have to do it alone. Through the pages of this book, I will be with you in shining new light into the dark places of your soul, and I will walk with you as you find hope, healing, courage, light, and peace.

Thank you so much for reading this book. It is my hope and prayer that it be a valuable companion for you on your recovery path, and that in these pages you find support to help rediscover your own greatness. I hope these words and exercises give you strength to heal your wounds, break free from your addiction, and unleash your inner freedom. That said, these exercises only work if you use them. Recovery is a lifelong journey of growth – there are no quick fixes, and I can't cure you of your addictions. Hopefully, I can guide you along the journey of recovery, and your own path will be uplifted, and your suffering will be lessened by these words.

I encourage you to read the whole book and return to it regularly. Take time to do the exercises I give you. The journey of recovery never ends, so you are welcome to read this book, and come back to it regularly. You can find links to additional resources on my website *www.andgodcreatedrecovery.com* Make sure you subscribe to the Our Jewish Recovery email list and join our Facebook community to find additional resources to support your journey, and encouragement, strength, and hope from others walking a recovery path.

Thank you for trusting me with your time, your energy, and for reading this book. There are so many books out there – I thank you for reading this one.

I pray that we are all guided to a better place, and that all who are in need of healing find the blessings of recovery, good health, love, serenity, and peace.

What is Addiction and How Do We Recover?

"The greatest hazard of all, losing one's self, can occur very quietly in the world, as if it were nothing at all." – Soren Kierkegaard[6]

Before we continue, let's take some time to understand what addiction is, and what it isn't, and how people can recover. Here are a few "textbook" definitions, and then we'll expand upon them.

According to the American Society of Addiction Medicine,

"addiction is a primary, chronic disease of brain reward, motivation, memory, and related circuitry. Dysfunction in these circuits leads to characteristic biological, psychological, social and spiritual manifestations. This is reflected in an individual pathologically pursuing reward and/or relief by substance use and other behaviors.

Addiction is characterized by inability to consistently abstain, impairment in behavioral control, craving, diminished recognition of significant problems with one's behaviors and interpersonal relationships, and a dysfunctional emotional response. Like other chronic diseases, addiction often involves cycles of relapse and remission. Without treatment or engagement in recovery activities, addiction is progressive and can result in disability or premature death.".[7]

According to Merriam Webster, to be an addict is "to devote or surrender oneself to something habitually or obsessively".[8] The root of addiction can also mean to be handed over or indebted to something. Addicts become enslaved to the substances and processes they use. Even knowing that the substance or process is bad for them, once the addiction is present, addicts are unable to stop the behavior, and will generally do anything they can to continue it.

What many people don't understand about addiction is that addictive behavior is a solution to an internal problem the addict can't or won't solve. For many people, it's a way of medicating an underlying condition that may not have been addressed. For others, what starts as a fun way to connect with others after school or work eventually spirals out of control.

The other important piece is that addiction is a disease of the brain. For too long we have treated addiction as if it were a moral failing, and the addicts are the sinners who have gone astray. Instead of moralizing, let us open our hearts with kindness and compassion, and help addicts find the treatment they need. Unfortunately, addiction is a progressive disease – left untreated, it only gets worse. It may feel like you can manage your disease on your own. You may not believe that anyone can help you. You may think you deserve your problems. I'm here to tell you that life can get better. **It's not your fault** you learned unhealthy behaviors and became an addict. We come by our wounds honestly. That said, **it is your responsibility to get clean and sober,**

11

and to become the best version of yourself, and I believe that the programs of recovery can help you do so. No one else can fix you, yet many of us will be happy to help and support you each step of the way.

Why do some people become addicts and others don't? Unfortunately, there is no satisfactory answer to this question as of yet. People can grow up in the same home and some will become addicts while others won't. Addiction often, though not always, runs in the family. Generally speaking, the more traumatic the childhood, the more likely someone is to need something to help them navigate their challenges, and if healthier options are not present, the child may learn to rely on unhealthy ones. This does not mean that if you had a difficult childhood you will automatically become an addict. Studies have shown that the more adverse childhood experiences, the greater the likelihood of medical challenges and addiction. You can take the ACE quiz and see for yourself if it applies to you.[9]

Addiction may also be caused by a healthy use of a prescription drug. If you are injured in a car accident, you may need pain medication to help you function. Over time, your body gets used to the medication, and you may need a higher dose just to get back to where you were on a lower dose. If you lose your health insurance or your doctor is no longer willing to write you a prescription, what do you do? You can try to find a new doctor, but maybe you can't get an

12

appointment for a while. The pain of withdrawal is so great that suddenly you're buying drugs on the street just to try and medicate your pain.

You may also have untreated depression or anxiety from your adverse life (childhood and/or adult) experiences. You may have an underlying medical condition that no one has treated you for, like bipolar or schizophrenia. If you've never been treated, you wouldn't know that there are other avenues of treatment available. You may just know that at a party someone handed you a pill, a cigarette, or a drink, you took it and felt better, and now you'll do anything to keep feeling that way, so that you don't have to feel the pain and misery of how you felt before.

There are two different types of addiction. The first is an addiction to a substance such as tobacco, alcohol, and drugs. The second is an addiction to a process or behavior, such as eating, sex, pornography, video games, internet use, working, exercising, shopping, cutting or harming one's body, gambling, and stealing. Some people are only addicted to one specific substance or behavior. Others, like me, are cross-addicted, which means we are addicted to multiple substances and processes. If I can't get a high from one addiction, I'll switch to another, and then another, until I finally feel numb or at peace. As we said above, left untreated, some people will just continue

13

managing their addictions for years. Some addicts are high-functioning and can do that. I was a full-time rabbi for six years and no one knew that behind the scenes I wasn't nearly as put-together as others thought. High-functioning addicts are all around us, living, as Thoreau wrote, "lives of quiet desperation". On the other hand, many addicts don't make it. We have over 175 overdoses a day. The economic toll is staggering. Too many lives are lost. How long will you wait before getting help? Why not make the first phone call today?

I can't emphasize strongly enough that **addiction is not a moral failing.** Addicts are too often blamed for not being able to discipline themselves better. If only they gave up their addictions, they are told, they would be happy and normal like everyone else. The craving is so strong that they can't just turn off the addiction. It must be treated, or the cycle will continue. The addict is in a constant search for the next hit of dopamine in the brain. The substances and processes they use become synonymous with relief, and the brain starts to crave the substances, which only spur the addictions on even further. In full-blown addiction, addicts frequently encounter relationship and legal problems. They don't always make good choices, and those loved ones who may have supported them earlier may need to take a step back in order to avoid enabling bad behavior. With a small support system, if any, addicts may find themselves on the streets, wondering how they got there and whether they can ever get out of the hell they find

themselves in.

Fortunately, the answer to that question is yes, if they are

willing to do the hard work necessary to get help and learn a healthier

way of living.

> "To counter the destructive consequences of addiction we draw
> on five major resources:
> 1) **Sobriety.** Our willingness to stop acting out in our own
>   personal bottom-line behavior on a daily basis.
> 2) **Sponsorship/Meetings**. Our capacity to reach for the
>   supportive fellowship within our recovery program
> 3) **Steps**. Our practice of the Twelve Step programs of
>   recovery to achieve emotional sobriety.
> 4) **Service.** Our giving back to the recovery community what
>   we continue to freely receive.
> 5) **Spirituality.** Our developing a relationship with a Power
>   greater than ourselves which can guide and sustain us in
>   recovery."[10]

These five resources have changed my life, and the life of so

many others in recovery. They are available for you as well. If you're

brand new to all of this, start by attending a meeting near you. You will

be amazed to find other people who have struggled with the same

problem you have. Like you, they have felt the pain of addiction. They

can show you the way forward and help you get there.

In order to break free of our addictions, we have to give up our

addictive habits and learn some new ones. In The Power of Habit: Why

We Do What We Do in Life and Business, Charles Duhigg says that a

habit is something we repeatedly do. Thank heavens for habits, because the brain can only hold so many pieces of information at a time.

Duhigg says it's seven, plus or minus two, depending on the situation.

Habits allow our brains to not have to work so hard and to retain more

information. When was the last time you thought about how to tie your

shoes? If we had to think about that every time we put our shoes on,

we'd spend way more time on that than we currently do. Habits save

time, and time is money and productivity. Unfortunately, they can also

keep us repeating addictive behavior. How does that happen?

> "The process within our brains is a three-step loop. First, there
> is a cue that tells your brain to go into automatic mode, and
> which habit to use. Then there is the routine, which can be
> physical or mental or emotional. Finally, there is a reward,
> which helps your brain figure out if this particular loop is worth
> remembering for the future. Over time, this loop – cue, routine,
> reward – becomes more and more automatic. The cue and
> reward become intertwined until a powerful sense of
> anticipation and craving emerges. Eventually…a habit is born."[11]

Addicts become so accustomed to their addictive behavior that

they don't even make conscious choices to indulge them, their brains

take over. What activities do you engage in habitually that could be

improved? Do you stare at your smartphone or turn on the television

every time you're bored? Do you reach for food or a bottle whenever

you're lonely?

Duhigg gives us what he calls the golden rule of

transformation. "If you use the same cue, and provide the same reward, you can shift the routine and change the habit. Almost any behavior can be transformed if the cue and reward stay the same."[12]

Instead of reaching for a bag of food when you're upset, call a friend. Instead of turning on the television, read a book. Go for a walk. Pray. Meditate. Exercise. Breathe. Feel your feelings. Laugh. Dance. Sit. Remember that the discomfort won't last forever.

According to Duhigg, there is a secret ingredient to change. The question is, if everyone wants to change, why are only a few able to do so? In America, we live in the most obese country in the world and in most cases it's not for lack of information – nobody wants to be obese. Nobody wants the long-term effects of being a cigarette smoker, gambler, addict. How is it that some people manage to change their habits, and some can't?

The answer is, that **in order to change a habit, you must believe that you can**. People who are down on their luck generally don't believe that they can change their situations. Everyone wants to be a millionaire, but when you're living paycheck to paycheck it's not easy to hold a vision of yourself as rich and successful. You don't have time to daydream. You need to work to live.

And for so many people, in a world which is too quick to judge and blame everyone for their imperfections regardless of how they acquired them, so many people spend their lives beating themselves up, refusing to believe that a better way is possible. I'm such a loser. I'll never amount to anything, so why bother trying? There's no use. And when we find ourselves without hope, without a reason to keep going, we turn to the quick fixes – alcohol, cigarettes, food, drugs, sugar, caffeine, gambling, sex, money, cars, television – anything to dull the pain and distract ourselves from ourselves.

I get it. Too many of us have been there. Too many of our young people end up dead from the toxic effects of the things they used to dull the pain. Too much time with their habits, not enough with a supportive, empowering community, not enough time believing in ourselves, challenging ourselves to grow.

My friends, I understand these realities. It's hard to change. It's painful to realize that the ways we've been living have led to negative consequences. It saddens us to think that we'll have to get rid of our favorite emotional crutch. That's why we need friends, who can lift us up when we're scared, who can remind us of all we've accomplished in life, and that we're strong enough to keep moving. We must believe in ourselves. If we're at war with ourselves, as so many people are, we'll never get very far. There's an African proverb I've heard that says, "if there's no enemy within, the enemy outside can do you no harm."

This is why **we can't recover on our own.** Addiction is too strong to face by ourselves. We need a supportive community to help us through the challenges. We need to be surrounded by people who will remind us that we are neither as messed up as we think, or as brilliant as we sometimes feel. We need others who will listen to our pain and our secrets and love us anyway.

In Chasing the Scream: The First and Last Days of the War on Drugs, Johann Hari writes that everything we think we know about addiction is wrong. Most addiction research is based off of studies that place a rat in a cage and give it two options of what to drink, water or water laced with diamorphine, which is heroin. In that experiment, the rat will always choose the water laced with heroin, over and over until it dies. Therefore, in order to cure addiction, we have to stop people from using addictive substances. If they just don't drink, smoke, or take drugs, all will be well.

That's a lovely theory, and certainly abstaining from the addictive substances is a laudable (and necessary) idea, but there's more to it than that. Professor Bruce Alexander noted that the rat is placed in the cage all alone. Of course, they drank the water with diamorphine in it, they had nothing else to do! He built what became known as Rat Park, with slides, cheese, and plenty of rats for company, everything a rat could want, to see if the rats would still choose to drink water laced with drugs over clean water if they weren't in the cage on their own. In his experiment, rats occasionally sipped on the drugged water, yet they didn't come back to it, they didn't overdose, and no one died. The same is true for humans. During the Vietnam War, twenty percent of American soldiers were using heroin. When they came back from the war, ninety-five percent of them went back to their communities and stopped using heroin on their own. Hospitals around the world give people diamorphine following surgery, and their medicine is much stronger than the heroin you can find on the street. The vast majority of people who leave hospitals after surgery go off their pain medications.

How does that happen? The answer, according to Bruce Alexander, is that **it's not the drugs that are the problem; it's the environment you live in.** Today, disconnection, isolation, and loneliness are at epidemic levels. We have fewer friends than we used to, and we communicate electronically instead of being nourished by in-person contact. We find ourselves frustrated, sad, depressed, and alone. It's no wonder that we think pills, foods, drinks, or other addictive behaviors might give our lives meaning and community. The truth is, addicts can certainly find community and connection in each other's company. It may not be healthy, but at least it's something to dull the pain and isolation.

According to Professor Alexander and Johann Hari, **"the opposite of addiction is not sobriety, it's connection".**[13] We humans are hard-wired to bond with others. If we can't do so, we will bond with things and suffer the consequences. Recovery gives us new habits, new community, and new hope for a better life.

In my life-coach training, I studied about the six human needs, and I recommend that you (and everyone) identify how these needs are manifesting in your life. Tony Robbins teaches that each of us has six human needs that drive our behavior, and we can measure our happiness and our overall wellbeing based on how well we are fulfilling our needs.

Those needs are:

"1) **Certainty** – assurance you can avoid pain and gain pleasure
2) **Uncertainty/Variety** – the need for the unknown, change, new stimuli
3) **Significance** – feeling unique, important, special, or needed
4) **Connection/Love** – a strong feeling of closeness or union with someone or something
5) **Growth** – an expansion of capacity, capability, or understanding
6) **Contribution** – a sense of service and focus on helping, giving to, and supporting others"[14]

These six human needs are driving our decisions each and every day. It may seem surprising when I say this, yet I know that **your addiction is meeting at least one need for you. The only problem is it's killing you in the process.** When I was in active addiction, I knew that food could make me feel better. I knew that pornography would get me to a state where I could forget the troubles of the world. I knew that gaming would give me a sense of accomplishment. Unfortunately, that sense is fleeting and doesn't ultimately contribute to the world or my own growth in a meaningful way. On the contrary, it distracts me from making a bigger contribution, and from finding the love and connection I seek.

Which needs is your addiction meeting? Be honest with yourself. Which needs are not being met? Are there healthier ways you can meet your needs than by engaging in addiction? Of course, there are. No one ever died from going to a meeting and sharing their emotions with a supportive group of others. Millions of people have died from thinking they can manage their addiction on their own.

In order to break the patterns of addiction, **we have to choose, each and every day to believe in our future and not give in to our struggles.** We have to know that we are created for a reason and that our life has meaning. We have to surround ourselves with others who can lift us up when we fall, and whose triumphs we can celebrate. When we find communities of connection, we can rely on them instead of on our addictions. I want that for you, for myself, and for everyone alive on this planet. **Everyone deserves to be happy, joyous, and free**. As we begin to free ourselves from the terrible consequences of addiction, we can look forward to helping others become free as well.

One day at a time, one step at a time, our future in sobriety is calling to us. Are you ready to answer the call?

It's Not Kosher for Jews To Be Addicts, Is It?

Whenever I teach about Judaism and recovery from addiction, people come up to me and thank me for doing so, since no one they know is talking about this Jewishly. Thankfully, there are a few others talking about recovery from a Jewish lens, yet too often Jews in recovery feel isolated from the Jewish world. When rabbis and Jewish leaders don't talk about the challenges of addiction, those of us in recovery feel that addiction must be treif (nonkosher), and outside the bounds of what's acceptable Jewish behavior. Somehow, we are not just addicts who have messed up our own lives; we've also become disappointments to our people, our history, our God, and the Jewish future. I'm aware that most rabbis and Jewish educators aren't trained in addiction, and don't know what to say. The smart rabbis and Jewish educators get trained to have at least a basic understanding of how addiction works and how Jews in recovery can be helped. Hopefully this book can help end the isolation that so many Jews feel.

The Jewish religion provides ample opportunities for healing and acquiring wisdom. Unfortunately, the legacy of trauma that Jews carry also means that we tend not to share our dirty laundry publicly. Our sons and daughters are supposed to become doctors and lawyers, not addicts in need of healing. We don't have these problems. Let the non-Jews worry about addiction; we'll be okay as we are. I remember a meeting of rabbis I was once invited to. A Jewish community leader had called us together to talk about how drugs were affecting the Jewish youth groups. Two Jewish teenagers were sent to rehab for drug addiction. Rabbis were asked to start talking about this publicly so that we could get people the help they needed. The silence of the rabbis in the room was deafening. They were ill equipped to talk about this, and uncomfortable that the issue was even raised. What were they supposed to do about it? One rabbi even went so far as to say that he wasn't hearing about any problems, so addiction must not exist in his community. I was shocked by the lengths he was willing to go to avoid having to address the reality that Jews, like everyone else on the planet, are affected by addiction.

There are actually quite a few sources in Jewish tradition talking about our interactions with alcohol, food, drugs, and other substances. The Bible itself contains episodes of drunkenness. The Talmud quotes Rabbi Meir as saying that "the tree that the first earthling ate from was a grape vine."[15] No wonder Adam and Eve were so tempted to break the one rule God had given them! Ten generations later, we read of Noah's actions following the flood. "And Noah, the man of the land, began and planted a vineyard. And he drank of the wine and was drunken; and he was uncovered within his tent."[16] Noah gets drunk and reveals his nakedness to others, and then curses his grandson for seeing him naked. Clearly Noah himself could've behaved better. Lot's daughters get him drunk, and sleep with him so that they can bear children.[17] Wine is intoxicating and has great power to affect our behavior.

In almost every Jewish holiday, we begin with blessings, including over wine. Wine or grape juice helps sanctify our time, making sure the holidays and Sabbaths will be sweet. On Purim we are commanded to be perfumed or spiced to such an extent that we can't know the difference between Mordechai and Haman. Many interpret the word perfumed to mean drunk or engaging in excess drinking. (Others say that taking a nap will suffice, though this is hardly a popular opinion). On Simchat Torah, perhaps the biggest Jewish celebration of the year when we finish reading the Torah and begin it again, many people will have a drink (or multiple drinks) to celebrate. On Passover, we're instructed to have four cups of wine. Many synagogues have kiddush or lechayim (to life!) clubs, where people will get together for a drink. The irony of saying "to life" before pouring a toxic substance into your body is noteworthy. Wine is the elixir of life! It helps everyone feel better, except when drunk to excess, it has terrible consequences. Scientists are actually rethinking how much alcohol is actually safe for human consumption. "Alcohol is a level-one carcinogen".[18] Even small amounts may be harmful to human health.

I don't drink wine or alcohol. I've never liked the taste and it seems silly for me to tempt myself with something else I might get addicted to. (And I never understood why I should spend time and money acquiring a taste for something either. If I don't like it now, will I really like it if I have a lot more of it?) There is often tremendous peer pressure in synagogues to join the kiddush club. "You don't drink, what's wrong with you?" "Come on, it won't hurt!" "Live a little." I always politely decline, yet it feels unsettling, as if they need me to join their drinking so they can feel validated in doing so. That's not a validation I'm willing to give (though I very much appreciate the synagogues that have made grape juice and other non-alcoholic beverages a regular part of their kiddush clubs).

I'm not going to tell you that any amount of wine is harmful and that we should never drink. Only you and your doctor can know how alcohol affects your system. I do find it interesting that even as

Jewish tradition finds many opportunities for us to drink alcohol, it also

recognizes that drinking too much causes problems.

Maimonides, the great Jewish philosopher, scholar, and physician said:

> "When the wise drinks wine he partakes only enough to moisten the food in his bowels; but whosoever intoxicates himself is a sinner, contemptible, and brings about the loss of his wisdom. If he intoxicates himself in the presence of the uncivilized, behold, this one blasphemed the Name" of God.[19]

Is it possible to rejoice on Jewish holidays without drinking to

excess? Of course. Commenting on the law that on Purim, we should

drink enough to not know the difference between the sinister Haman

and praiseworthy Mordechai, the Chofetz Chaim, scholar, ethicist, and

one of the early influences of the Mussar movement, wrote:

> "We should not become drunk and demean ourselves by rejoicing. We are not commanded to rejoice for the sake of debauchery and stupidity, rather we should rejoice with a delight that leads us to love G-d and acknowledge the miracles wrought for us."[20]

How much wine is too much to handle?

> "On the topic of drinking wine, Rabba bar Rav Huna said: One who has drunk wine, must not pray, but if he nonetheless prayed, his prayer is a prayer, i.e. he has fulfilled his obligation. On the other hand, one who is intoxicated with wine must not pray, and if he prayed, his prayer is an abomination. One of them opened the discussion and said: What are the circumstances where a person is considered one who has drunk wine, and what are the circumstances where a person is considered one who is intoxicated with wine? One who has drunk wine refers to anyone who has drunk wine but whose mind remains clear enough that he is able to talk in the presence of a king. One who is intoxicated refers to anyone

who is so disoriented by the wine he has drunk that he is not able to talk in the presence of a king."[21]

Unfortunately, getting drunk often leads to inappropriate behavior. The Talmud relates that

> "Rabba and Rabbi Zeira prepared a Purim feast with each other, and they became intoxicated to the point that Rabba arose and slaughtered Rabbi Zeira. The next day, when he became sober and realized what he had done, Rabba asked God for mercy, and revived him. The next year, Rabba said to Rabbi Zeira: Let the Master come and let us prepare the Purim feast with each other. He said to him: Miracles do not happen each and every hour, and I do not want to undergo that experience again."[22]

Even Rabbis and Torah scholars can fall victim to the consequences of alcohol. Rabba, pleading for God's mercy, brought Rabbi Zeira back to life. We don't have that power today, yet the risks of overdose and fatality are just as real today as they were then. Drugs are just as bad. "If you take drugs, you will become addicted and you will squander away your money."[23]

What about drugs? Are we allowed to consume things that aren't good for us? Rabbi Elliot Dorff, a noted Conservative rabbi and bioethicist, writes:

> "Judaism allows Jews to ingest many things that are not intrinsically holy as part of the effort to fulfill the responsibility to maintain a healthy body, mind and soul, and furthermore, as part of enjoying God's bounty, even when not directly related to matters of health...Whether using marijuana recreationally fits into that Jewish description of the nature and purpose of

life depends on what its effects turn out to be. If it decreases pain in dying patients, then one not only may, but must, work to make it legally available to them. Thus, in sum, marijuana in and of itself is not inherently bad or good; it must be judged in terms of its effects in creating a kingdom of priests and a holy nation.[24]

For Rabbi Dorff, so long as a substance helps us be holy, it's

permitted, otherwise it's forbidden.

Rabbi Moshe Feinstein argues against the growing trend of marijuana usage by yeshiva students.

> "Behold, with regard to certain yeshiva students who have begun smoking hash (marijuana), It is obviously forbidden to smoke marijuana, as this violates many basic laws of our Torah.
>
> First of all, it physically injures the person. Even if there are people who are not physically affected by this, it mentally affects the person as it destroys his mind and prevents him from understanding things properly. This is a terrible thing, since not only can the individual not properly study Torah, he also can not pray and properly perform Mitzvot (commandments), since doing them mindlessly is considered as if they were not done at all.
>
> Furthermore, he is creating within himself a very strong desire (addiction), which is much stronger than the desire to eat, etc. which is necessary for a person to live. There are many that cannot control and withstand this desire. This is a very grave prohibition, as we find that a Wayward and Rebellious Son [is killed] (See Deuteronomy 21:18) for creating within himself a very strong desire, even though it is to eat kosher food! How much more so it is forbidden for a person to bring upon himself an even greater desire, especially for something that a person does not need at all...
>
> Additionally, the parents of the person smoking are certainly pained by his actions, in which case he is violating the Mitzvah of Kibbud Av V'Em (honoring one's father and mother). He is also violating the Mitzvah of "Kedoshim Ti'Hiyu" (You shall

be holy), as explained by the Ramban in his commentary on the Chumash (5 Books of Moses). This also leads him to transgress other prohibitions, besides the actual prohibition of taking drugs. The bottom line is that it is clear and obvious that this is one of the grave prohibitions, and everyone must try with all of their strength to remove this impurity (Tuma'ah) from all Children of Israel."[25]

If alcohol and drugs are bad, what about food? We need to eat

food to live, and yet, that too can become problematic.

"Gluttonous eating is like a deadly poison for every person and it is the essence of all the sicknesses. And most sicknesses that come to a person are only because of bad foods or because he fills his stomach and engages in gluttonous eating, even if it is of good foods."[26]

Rabbi Adin Steinsaltz had an interesting approach to

addressing the question of addiction. "If you are the master, fine. If you

are the slave, then you are in trouble no matter what you're the slave of,

whether it be coffee, exercise or Torah study."[27] Rabbi Steinsaltz

understood that we can become subservient to anything. Once we do,

it's very hard to get out of the throes of addiction.

The Talmudic rabbis (and many since) said that a commitment

to Jewish life can save us from our addictions.

"Once there was a man who was very careful in his observance of the mitzvah of tzitzit [the prayer shawl worn by many observant Jews every day]. He heard there was a prostitute in a distant town who accepted four hundred gold pieces for her services. He sent her four hundred gold pieces and made an appointment. When the appointed time came, he went and sat at her door. "Enter," she said, and he entered. She made him seven beds, six of silver and the seventh of gold, with a silver ladder between each bed, and to the top one, a golden ladder.

She went up and sat unclothed on the uppermost bed, and he ascended to sit beside her. Suddenly the four fringes of his tzitzit brushed against his face and he slipped down and sat on the ground. She slipped down after him and sat beside him.

"By the Roman emperor," she demanded, "I won't let you leave until you tell me what blemish you saw in me!"

"By the service of God," he replied, "never have I seen a woman as beautiful as you. But there is one mitzvah that God has commanded us called tzitzit, and regarding it, twice it is written 'I am Hashem your God' (Bamidbar 15:41), I am the God who will punish and the God who will reward, and [the four fringes of my tzitzit] will be as four witnesses against me."

She said to him: "I won't let you go until you tell me your name, the name of your city, the name of your rabbi, and the name of the Beit Midrash [study hall] where you study Torah." He wrote it down and put it in her hand. She then divided all her possessions – a third she gave to the kingdom, a third to the poor, and a third she kept for herself – except for her beds and bedding and came to the Beit Midrash of Rabbi Chiya.

She said to him, "Rabbi, instruct me and I shall be a convert." He questioned her, "My daughter, might you have laid eyes on one of my students?" She showed him the note in her hand. He said to her, "Go and enjoy your claim."

The same beds which she had spread for him illicitly she now spread for him permissibly."[28]

I love this story, and especially the image of the tzitzit

smacking him down the ladder and preventing him from sleeping with

the prostitute, which leads to her joining the Jewish people and

marrying him. Clearly Jewish wisdom can save us from our follies and

redeem us from the poor decisions we make. No sin is irreparable. We

can always find a way back, and Torah study and observance of mitzvot (commandments) can save us from harm (though if we're addicted to something, Torah study alone is not the answer. Proper medical guidance is always a key component of a recovery program).

Here's the ultimate question for rabbis – can one be addicted to learning Torah? Apparently so!

> "The mishna stated: For sailors, the set interval for conjugal relations is once every six months. This is the statement of Rabbi Eliezer. Rav Berona said that Rav said: The halakha (legal ruling) is in accordance with the opinion of Rabbi Eliezer. Rav Adda bar Ahava said that Rav said: This is the statement of Rabbi Eliezer, but the Rabbis say: Students may leave their homes to study Torah for as long as two or three years without permission from their wives. Rava said: The Sages relied on Rabbi Adda bar Ahava's opinion and performed an action like this themselves, but the results were sometimes fatal.
>
> This is as it is related about Rav Rehumi, who would commonly study before Rava in Mehoza: He was accustomed to come back to his home every year on the eve of Yom Kippur. One day he was particularly engrossed in the halakha he was studying, and so he remained in the study hall and did not go home. His wife was expecting him that day and continually said to herself: Now he is coming, now he is coming. But in the end, he did not come. She was distressed by this and a tear fell from her eye. At that exact moment, Rav Rehumi was sitting on the roof. The roof collapsed under him and he died. This teaches how one must be careful, as he was punished severely for causing anguish to his wife, even inadvertently."[29]

As wonderful as Torah study can be, if it is done to the detriment of our family obligations, that is too much, and at least in this story, can lead to death.

33

We must take care of our loved ones, and we must take care of

ourselves as well. "וְנִשְׁמַרְתֶּם מְאֹד לְנַפְשֹׁתֵיכֶם - And you shall guard lives

very well"[30], says the Torah. While originally referencing idolatry, this

verse has become a central teaching that taking care of our bodies and

our souls is a Jewish requirement. A story is told of Rabbi Aryeh Leib

Halberstam, the Sanzer Rebbe, who, at the end of his life, was ill, and

doctors told him that he could no longer eat maror, bitter herbs, on

Passover, under any circumstances. How could a holy rebbe not fulfill

the commandment to eat maror? When it came time for the eating of

the maror, he lifted it up and said:

"בָּרוּךְ אַתָּה ה', אֱלֹקֵינוּ מֶלֶךְ הָעוֹלָם
אֲשֶׁר קִדְּשָׁנוּ בְּמִצְווֹתָיו וְצִוָּנוּ וְנִשְׁמַרְתֶּם מְאֹד לְנַפְשֹׁתֵיכֶם."

"Blessed are You, Lord our God, King of the universe, who has
sanctified us with Your commandments, and commanded us to
guard our lives with great care."[31]

I love this new blessing he created. Jewish tradition wants us to

bless everything we eat or drink. If that's the case shouldn't there also

be a blessing for not eating things that might do us harm? This is a

wonderful blessing to say every time we think about giving in to our

addictions and don't. Thanks, God, for giving us the wisdom to take

care of ourselves!

Maimonides and others would agree that taking care of our health is crucial, and a requirement for all members of the Jewish people.

> "Since a healthy and whole body is necessary for the ways of God (for it is impossible to imply or know anything of Godly wisdom when one is sick), therefore one must distance himself from things that are damaging to the body and to accustom oneself to things that strengthen and make one healthy. They are as follows: a person should only eat when he is hungry, and drink when he is thirsty, and not delay his orifices even for one second..."[32]

Do you eat more than you need? Do you drink to excess? **Do you guard over your body and soul with great care or do you put yourself at risk unnecessarily?** Do you appreciate that your body is a gift from the Holy One, to be treated as a priceless work of art? How can you have even more respect for yourself? How can you show yourself more compassion, and make sure you are taking good care of yourself?

The Mussar tradition supports our staying abstinent. Rabbi Moshe Chaim Luzzato said that "in order to attain holiness, it is essential for a person to practice abstinence."[33] Rabbeinu Yonah of Gerondi added that it is wise to "eat only enough to satisfy your own hunger and you will protect yourself from trouble and preserve your health. Do not keep eating as long as the food still appeals to you, because the palate always wants more until the stomach is loaded.

Eating like this will lead to all sorts of damage and disease."[34] Rabbi Bahya ibn Pakuda wrote that "when the evil inclination overwhelms your reason and entices you, it steers you toward excess, which brings you to ruin and destroys your body. You need to abstain from the things that please and relax you to maintain balance."[35] When we use to excess, our bodies suffer the consequences.

The Talmud cites the following: "The Holy One, Blessed be God, loves three people: One who does not get angry; one who does not get drunk; and one who is forgiving."[36] Obviously, Jewish tradition would prefer that none of us become addicts, none of us drink, smoke, eat, gamble or do anything to excess. That being said, our tradition constantly reminds us that **we can always take another step closer to God, and whenever we do, God will turn towards us as well. Wherever you are on your recovery path, now is a great time to take another action in your healing.** If you've struggled with the idea that Jews can't be addicts, apparently the history of our people contains many examples of struggle with food, drink, sex, too much studying and other compulsive behaviors. Today, may we be strengthened, may we be blessed, may we grow into the next phase of our recovery, turning over a new leaf in support of our journey to heal our lives and get closer to God. It's not un-kosher for Jews to be addicts. Jews (and non-Jews) have struggled with addiction for thousands of years. It may

36

feel isolating and lonely to be a Jew in recovery, yet there are more Jewish addicts out there than you might think. **We who are in recovery have a special opportunity to begin our lives anew each day. With God's help, we will discover the courage and strength to chart a new path of healing and sobriety, one day at a time.**

My Recovery Story

How I did become an addict? What gives me the holy chutzpah to write this book? Here are some highlights of my own journey.

I was born September 20, 1979 in Grand Rapids, Michigan. My father was a synagogue rabbi in the Conservative movement, my mother was a Hebrew School and Jewish day school teacher and principal. They instilled many Jewish values in me – observing Shabbat, keeping kosher, giving Tzedakah, being kind to all in need, and many more. I grew up in synagogues, Jewish day school, Jewish summer camp, and Jewish youth groups. Judaism was a way of life, and a source of pride in our household. From the outside looking in, we were a family to emulate, and a source of pride in the community.

From the inside looking out, there was a lot left to be desired.

My older brother Avi was born in 1977. My mother was jaundiced after giving birth to him. Doctors were unsure why. She would eventually be diagnosed with ulcerative colitis and schlerosang cholangitis. She may also have had Crohn's; they were never quite sure. She was twenty-seven at the time, and I can only imagine how she must have felt when they told her that her life would never be the same, and that due to her illness, she shouldn't have more children, and probably wouldn't live to see her thirtieth birthday. She wanted more children, and she didn't want Avi to be an only child, especially if she was going to die early. I was born healthy and mom survived childbirth as determined as ever to keep living each and every day to its' fullest.

We left Grand Rapids when I was nine months old and moved to Nashville, Tennessee, where my sister Shoshi was born. When I was five, we moved again to Princeton, New Jersey where my brother Rafi was born. We spent four months in Jerusalem when I was 12, came back to Princeton, finished the school year, celebrated my Bar Mitzvah, and moved the next day to London, Ontario, where we spent three years, after which we moved to Fairfax, Virginia, where I finished high school. (Everyone always wants to know where I am from. I have no idea).

Home life was not the happiest environment. My parents were often at odds with each other, shouting at each other, and letting their tempers get the best of them. My mother's illnesses often landed her in the hospital, and I can remember more than a few times when I'd come home from school to find that mom had been taken to the hospital. In addition to her liver problems, she also battled cancer on five different occasions. She was no stranger to chemotherapy, radiation, hospitals, pharmacies, doctors' offices, and through it all she somehow managed to put food on the table most nights and make sure we had clothes, doctors, and enough to get by. She was unrelenting in her desire to keep working and providing for her family and the students she taught. She would be at the doctor's office for chemo at six in the morning, so that she could be ready at seven-thirty to greet the students as they entered the school. She used to say she had two speeds in life: fast-forward and reverse. When she was well, she was almost always busy, yet when she was sick, she suffered tremendously. She was angry and resentful of her body failing her. She tried so hard to push herself. I'm sure she knew that her body wouldn't last forever, and I know she was scared of dying without seeing her children happy and successful. She tried to make the most she could with the time she had left. Every day is a blessing, she'd say, even when those days have too much struggle and pain.

Unfortunately, her disappointment at moving every few years and her inability to stay healthy led to her not having the emotional space to be present for myself and my siblings (I'm sure synagogue and school politics didn't help either). She was adamant in her demand that we be as perfect as possible, and we knew that everything we did would be a reflection of her and dad. Bringing shame to the family name was one of the worst things we could do, and if we ever came close, she was not shy about telling us how we disappointed her. I'm all for having high standards, and yet her approach taught me that anything less than perfection was a complete failure.

I remember coming home with a ninety-eight on a test. I was proud of having done so well. When I showed it to her, without batting an eye or offering any congratulations, she immediately said: "What'd you miss?" I was crushed. I wondered what more I could possibly do to earn her love. What on earth did I do wrong to deserve her harsh treatment of me? Mom taught me and my siblings to cook, clean, and do laundry. I remember a moment in high school where I came home and saw that there were a few loads of laundry to do. I put the towels in the wash. She came home a bit later and immediately yelled at me for not having thrown the darks in instead. How I was supposed to know that she wanted the darks in I have no idea. Why she couldn't have thanked me for throwing the towels in and asked me to put the darks in next, I also don't know.

I lived in fear of my mother. She yelled at me and my siblings for the slightest things which disappointed her. I remember her telling us that she worked so hard at school and she pushed herself so much that she didn't have the space to deal with us when she got home. There is no question that she loved us, and she did sometimes offer compliments. I knew, however, that I couldn't rely on her for my emotional needs. I saw her be kind and caring to her students and faculty and people in the congregations. When she got home, she wasn't nearly as kind to her family.

Dad wasn't happy at home either. Mom yelled at him, he'd yell back, they'd both get upset and we'd be caught in the middle. Dad withdrew and focused on congregational work. His father died when he was twelve, and while I'm sure he did the best he could to be a good father, looking back it's clear he didn't know what he was doing, and he often didn't have the emotional space for us either. The politics and pressures of congregational life are challenging and exhausting. I'm sure he wanted to be more present in our lives, and home wasn't a happy place for him either.

Almost every child wants to be like their parents, at least in some ways. I took to leading services, reading from the Torah, teaching adult education even while I was in High School, and being involved in social action activities. Some part of me thought that if I did those things maybe my parents would love me more. Maybe if I did a lot of cooking and cleaning around the house I wouldn't get yelled at. Maybe I'd have deep friendships at the synagogue or in youth group which would take me out of the house as much as possible.

I had a lot of challenges in school. I would be the best student in class, participating regularly, and yet when it came to tests and writing papers, I had a hard time focusing and would put so much pressure on myself to make everything perfect that I would prevent myself from getting assignments done. What did I know about these topics anyway? Who was I to write a report? It'll probably not be any good and I'll just get yelled at anyway so why even bother? I couldn't handle the internal pressure to conform to my mother's high expectations. I wouldn't turn in homework, and then I'd lie and say I'd forgotten it at home, or that the teacher had lost it. In reality of course I hadn't done the homework and was trying to buy myself extra time. When my parents found out I'd be yelled at even more. They didn't understand that yelling at me would only compound how worthless I already felt (and in a dysfunctional way, at least when they were yelling at me, I had their attention). It was clear to me that I was giving my parents a bad name, and not living up to their idealized image of me as their perfect son. I wish they had sat me down and asked me what was wrong and gotten me the help I needed. I was scared, sad, and lonely.

The only way I knew to be comforted was to eat. Eating would distract me from my pain and make me feel better. My mother was a fabulous baker, and her challahs and desserts were legendary. Cookies, cakes, pies, brownies, and much more were found in our kitchen. She found baking therapeutic. When my siblings and I had our bar and bat mitzvahs, mom baked all of the desserts for the Friday night dinner,

Saturday lunch, Saturday night party, and Sunday morning brunch, and because we were a rabbinic family we invited the whole congregation to our celebrations – I think there were 700 people at my bar mitzvah. She baked a lot, and she and dad taught us that there was no emotion that couldn't be solved with the right amount of sugar. Feeling sad? Have a cookie. Really upset? Have a piece of cake? Majorly ticked off? Bake something and then eat it. Desserts were always plentiful in the house, and since I knew that I couldn't bring my emotional needs to mom or dad, when I was upset the only thing I knew how to do was eat. Mom was allowed to express her emotions in the house, and she made it clear on several occasions that her body failing her was a real thing to be sad about. The rest of us just needed to snap out of our lethargy and be happy already, or at the very least stop expressing our own sadness, since it was getting in the way of her misery.

So instead of turning to mom or dad when I was upset, I turned to food. I was the one who would finish everyone else's food at the end of the meal – there were starving children in Africa and we couldn't let food go to waste (how my eating more would help them I never actually understood). I ate and I ate, and I ate some more. Food made me feel better, and I could finish everyone else's meal – I was good at something! Unfortunately, I also gained a lot of weight because of how much I ate, and mom then yelled at me for being fat. I didn't want to

44

turn into my fat father, did I? Of course, I was already sad at being overweight, she didn't need to remind me. I wasn't good at sports, and my parents didn't exercise. Sometimes I rode my bicycle in high school, but a regular form of exercise was not part of my upbringing.

I didn't have many friends growing up – moving every few years didn't help. I was shy and afraid of being judged or being seen for the miserable screw-up I thought I was. If only I did better at school, if only I managed things better around the house, if only I anticipated everything mom wanted before she wanted it then she wouldn't yell at me and I'd be okay. If only I led services, read Torah, and volunteered at the synagogue more maybe dad would notice me, and we could spend more time together. If only...

I had a number of medical challenges. As a child I wet the bed a lot, which was embarrassing on sleepovers and at summer camp. Asthma and sleep apnea meant I didn't breathe or sleep well, and I was exhausted all the time until I finally was tested and started using a CPAP machine to help me sleep better. Doctors found an irregular heartbeat when I was in high school, which explained why I used to sweat all the time and why I'd get dizzy when I stood up too fast. I had severe allergies, flat feet, poor breathing, was out of shape, and often had a hard time moving without wheezing. But other than that, I was okay…I mean, what did I have to complain about? Mom's problems were worse than mine.

We didn't have much money growing up. We always had enough to eat, but my parents were often yelling at each other about money. I learned that there was never enough money, though if mom yelled at dad long enough and loud enough, he would come around and money could be found for the high school trip or other expense he thought was too extravagant. My parents both engaged in retail therapy, my mother buying herself new clothes and shoes, and my father buying books to read. I remember a visit with dad and my siblings to the bookstore. He told us we could each pick out one or two books. When it was time to check out, he purchased about ten. The message seemed clear – there was always money for him to buy what he wanted, the rest of us had to make do with scraps. While I'm sure it wasn't his intention, I internalized that I wasn't worth spending money on. I wasn't important enough to be valuable.

I don't want it to sound like my parents were terrible people. They were normal, flawed human beings doing the best they could, who found the toll of life to be too much to carry. Being a congregational rabbi is a challenging profession. Being a school principal isn't easy either. I know it couldn't have been easy for either of them to deal with synagogue and school politics, my mother's health, moving every few years, or their four children and two miscarriages. They worried constantly about synagogue politics and made the mistake of talking about congregants around the dinner table, telling us afterwards that we couldn't tell anyone what mom and dad actually thought about them, since if they did, dad could get fired and we'd have to move again. And mom didn't want anyone to know how sick she was so we couldn't talk about that either.

There was no question I was loved. Unfortunately, in my young mind, love became synonymous with sadness and pain. As I got older, I saw my classmates being interested in romance. My parents never told me how to ask someone out on a date or how to be in a relationship. The first time I heard my dad talk about sex (aside from when they were yelling at each other) was in front of my youth group. I was mortified. And mom made it clear that my job in life was to find and marry a nice Jewish woman, put her on a pedestal and give her everything she wants, because men are schmucks and I'd be worthless without a woman by my side. How to find this person, what to say to them, and how to make any of that happen I never knew and she never said. I was incredibly shy, and I certainly wasn't going to bring someone home to the house. I accepted that I should find the woman of my dreams, though I couldn't understand if I was a schmuck on my own, why would anyone want to date me? Lots of my youth group friends were dating. I was too shy. I hung out with other awkward kids who would somehow all have to go to the bathroom or get another drink when it came time for the slow dances. Sigh. I felt pathetic – I was a nice guy, why couldn't I have a girlfriend? What was wrong with me that I hadn't already found the woman to marry? Did everyone find me as wanting as I found myself?

In eighth grade a girl asked me out – what she saw in me I haven't a clue. I didn't think she was marriage material, so I turned her down. Can you imagine the absurdity of thinking she wasn't marriage material in eighth grade, before even getting to know her? That same year, the guys in my class discovered pornography in a garbage can. We all looked. It was possibly the first time I'd ever seen a woman's naked body. Everyone ogled and eventually they threw it back in the garbage and left. I took it out of the garbage and brought it home. I was hooked. There were stories of romance and pictures of beautiful women. My hormones were developing, and I discovered masturbation. I was too shy to date, but I fantasized that the women in the magazine were interested in me. There was a bookstore across the street from my high school. I would go after school sometimes and sneak pornography into my jacket. I couldn't possibly pay for it – somebody might see me, and my parents might find out! I stole from the bookstore, feeling guilty and ashamed of myself, and desperate for at least the false sense of connection I felt with the women in the magazines.

My only saving grace in high school was music. I had taken drum lessons since third grade. In eighth grade my classmates and I formed a band to play two songs at our graduation. Several of us continued as My Brother's Kippah Klezmer Band, playing at Jewish community events and at the high school. I loved making music with others. I was in the high school orchestra, and later in jazz band too. I felt that when I was drumming, I was at peace, as if the music were washing over me, and other people were enjoying our music. It got me out of the house and allowed me to help other people feel good, and while it was not always easy, being in a band allowed me to form some deeper friendships. I listened to and played a lot of music in those days. Music has been a big part of my life ever since.

Somehow, by the grace of God I made it out of high school. I didn't really know anything about college. All I knew is that I wanted to apply to a school with a big Jewish population. I applied to Brandeis University, where my older brother went. I applied to the Joint Program between Columbia University and List College of the Jewish Theological Seminary (aka JTS), where both my parents spent their college years. My mother insisted I apply to a third school, so I applied to Brown University – there was a cute girl in my youth group who got in there and that seemed as good a reason as any to pick a school. I knew I wouldn't get in to Brown. Brandeis and the Joint Program both accepted me. The Joint Program offered more money than Brandeis, so the decision was made. I thought I would do the Joint Program and then stay at JTS for their rabbinical program, as my father had done years before. New York City, here I come, everything will be great in school, right? Not exactly.

I loved a lot of my college years, made some great friends, and took wonderful classes. I was very active with the Columbia University Hillel, volunteering with KOACH, the Conservative group on campus, drumming in the Klezmer Band and in a rock group called Damn the Core, serving as a hunger and homelessness intern with the JTS Va'ad Gemilut Hasadim (Office of Community Outreach), organized a few music festivals for Jewish college groups, and more. I spent two summers volunteering in Israel with Danny Siegel and the Ziv Tzedakah Fund, providing funds to people doing amazing justice work in Israel, and educating American youth group participants on why social justice was important from a Jewish perspective and how to do it themselves. I loved it, and Danny became a friend and mentor, and remains so to this day.

My teachers at JTS were incredible, and I loved learning about Jewish history, literature, theology, Bible, Talmud, and more. At

Columbia, I was a comparative literature major – I had always enjoyed reading growing up and it seemed like something I could handle. Unfortunately, my academic challenges followed me to college, and I had the same challenges writing papers. My mother's health was also worsening, and I was worried about her, and still enmeshed in her life, trying from a distance to help her, returning on school breaks (when she'd often end up in the hospital, leaving me to teach her classes), and still seeking her approval. I was kicked out of Columbia twice, for not writing papers, and for lying about why to the teachers and to the Dean. I knew I couldn't tell the truth – if I did, they'd see me for the miserable failure I was, and I'd upset my mother, who's wrath I would feel even from a distance. I didn't understand why I was having so many problems, and I accepted that it was all my fault. If only I studied harder, if only I pushed myself harder. My mom pushed herself, what was wrong with me that I couldn't do the same? I was struggling to hold on, wondering if I'd lose it all.

A Bible teacher at JTS saw I was struggling and suggested to me that I see a friend of hers for counseling. My parents agreed that it was wise, and I spent a few years in therapy, which quite possibly saved my life. I started learning how to set boundaries with my parents, and I started to understand that desperately trying to gain my mother's approval was only pushing me further down the rabbit hole of guilt and shame. My therapist was one of the first people to actually listen to my thoughts. She gave me hope that I could get through my problems and find better ways to live.

When I was twenty, the world gave me an opportunity that would change my life. I was in my dorm room, sitting at my desk, and got an email stating that a new organization was starting out called Hazon. Their first project was a cross-USA Jewish environmental bike ride from Seattle to D.C., about 3400 miles over the course of ten weeks. I still don't know why, but as I read the email describing the trip, I knew I had to do it. I didn't know anything about the outdoors. I don't know that I'd ever been camping. I was not in shape and probably hadn't ridden a bicycle in a few years. And yet, the light bulb inside my head went off and told me I needed to do this. My friends thought I was crazy for wanting to do it. My parents wanted me to get a job that summer so I could help pay for college. I told them I needed to do this to find myself, and they said they thought I'd already done that the year before in Israel. I wanted their blessing to go on the trip. I'm not sure they could wrap their minds around it as it was so far out of their (and my!) comfort zones. I went anyway.

On the trip I discovered the outdoors and the beauty of America. I connected to God and spirituality in nature. I found a new group of friends and I embraced the mission of caring for the earth, even becoming vegan (for thirteen years) on the day we visited a kosher slaughterhouse in Postville, Iowa. I pushed myself on that ride. I still remember the pain of my thighs burning those first few days. Ouch! Yet I also remember that by the second week I was up to eighty-five miles in one day, and managed a few century days, riding over a hundred miles. And what a rush it is to soar down the Rocky Mountains! Wheeeeeeee! My top speed was 42.5 miles per hour, which broke the car speed limit! There was no way to slow down so I was just holding on. What fun! That trip taught me that I could achieve big things for myself. I'm not honestly sure I knew that beforehand. It is not easy to cycle across the country. It takes a lot of time, effort, energy, and a willingness to keep going even when you're sore, even when you're riding into the wind, and in the rain and cold. It takes determination and it takes a sense of adventure, which I've thankfully always had. The sense of accomplishment I got from the trip was powerful. I bicycled across the country! I knew that I wanted to get back to the outdoors, and I would continue riding with Hazon for years after, in their New York, DC, and Israel rides.

I returned to New York, ready for school, or so I thought.

And yet, life was still too much. Dad flew up from Florida, where he'd taken an interim pulpit, and then stayed on at the congregation. Mom was still in New Jersey and they were visiting back and forth every few weeks. He told me he and mom were getting divorced. I was crushed. So was she. They had a very bitter divorce, and often put my siblings and me in the middle. In retrospect, they probably should've gotten divorced well before they did. There were times growing up when mom left the house, saying she wasn't coming back, and she always did. He left once or twice and came back too. (I even walked out a few times, but there was no place I could go but home.) They told themselves they were staying in it for the sake of the children, and he didn't want to be the one to leave a sick wife. Once they were apart, I think he enjoyed being free of mom's questioning his every move and saw that he could have a better life without her. I'm sure it was a difficult decision for him. I wish they could've settled amicably and not taken their frustrations out on my siblings and me. If only…

My second year of college I started dating someone. My pornography use came to college with me, and yet I still knew I was supposed to find someone to marry. She was a senior, and we connected over some social action work we were both involved in. She seemed very nice, took an interest in me, and we started spending time together, and then dating. That was my first romantic relationship. We were together for four and a half years. She stuck by me when after getting tossed from school the second time I had a nervous breakdown and I needed to take time off of school to recover. I spent a painful few months with my mother and younger siblings in New Jersey, and eventually made it back to school, transferring my Columbia studies over to City College. At City College, I was sent for educational testing to see if I learned differently. Lo and behold the test showed that while I do very well in certain areas, I am poorer in others. My oral comprehension is better than most, my visual comprehension is challenging, possibly because of my lazy eye. Most people have two eyes that look generally in the same direction. My left eye is lazy so it's sometimes hard to focus on big blocks of text. I learned that I was both gifted and had special needs when it came to academic learning. The lies I had believed about being a moron and needing to work harder were revealed. I didn't need to work harder – I needed to understand how I could learn in a way that works for me. Once I understood that, I did much better at City College and at JTS. It wasn't easy, but I had more compassion for myself, and the teachers were willing to work with me and adjust accordingly when needed.

Later on, I noticed a pattern when I was dating. When I was with my girlfriend, I felt okay in my own skin. When we were apart, I felt pretty miserable and would agonize until she came back. I fell head over heels in love with her pretty quickly. She was the one, she had to be! Finally, I can get married and have someone who loves me, and I'll be happy. That I had asked her to marry me amidst my nervous breakdown was probably a sign I wasn't in great shape. She said yes, and eventually came to realize our dynamic wasn't healthy. I was devastated when she ended it. It felt like the world as I knew it was over. I was alone, adrift, and didn't know how to function on my own. Looking back, I know she made the right decision. I was a mess and I was using my relationship with her as a way to prop myself up, to tell myself I was worth something to someone. I felt rejected by her. What was wrong with me that she ended it? And what could possibly be wrong with her that she was willing to give up on our dreams? I was miserable.

My mother's health was deteriorating, and her doctors determined she needed a liver transplant. The Mayo clinic in Jacksonville, Florida was willing to treat her. She went down for extensive testing and they approved her to be on their waiting list. Unfortunately, the insurance company, which had paid for the testing, then declared that the transplant would be experimental (despite what the doctors said) and refused to pay for it. We were devastated. There was no question mom would die without a new liver. What could we possibly do?

Another miracle happened. Our friend Danny Siegel stepped in and said that he and the Ziv Tzedakah Fund would help raise the money. Fundraising letters went out to every Jewish listserve we could think of, and unbelievably the Jewish world was moved to act. Within a week we had enough donations to cover the transplant! We were amazed. Mayo had never seen anything like it. My grandmother flew down with mom to Jacksonville, and seventeen days later she received her new liver. We were thrilled and she was able to go back home and back to work shortly thereafter.

I finished most of my schooling and then wondered what to do with myself next. I'd had enough of New York City and wasn't ready for rabbinical school. Every Labor Day Hazon does a weekend retreat and bike ride into New York. There were always young Jewish environmental educators from the Teva Learning Center, based at Isabella Freedman Retreat Center in Falls Village, Connecticut, and a friend posted that Teva was looking for more educators. The light bulb again went off, and I became a Teva educator for two years, working with Jewish day school students and synagogue groups to learn about the environment and Jewish teachings about caring for the earth. My office was five hundred acres of forest. I got to teach every day, sing, and make a difference in the lives of our students. I loved almost every minute of Teva. Being connected to nature was a boon to my spirit. Making music and sharing holy community with others was a true gift. When I started at Teva I had just broken up with my girlfriend. The

Teva staff welcomed me in and essentially said that they didn't care how messed up I thought I was, they were just going to spread love and hold me tight, and it worked.

I was still using food to mask my emotions. My pornography usage went way down. I dated a few Teva and Adamah (a Jewish farming fellowship program also at Isabella Freedman) staff. When I was dating, I again wanted to be close to them at all times. On my own I was much sadder than when I was with them. I didn't quite know why. I became the lead educator at Teva, helping train the new staff in educational theory and Jewish wisdom. Those two years were powerful and healing. I loved hiking every day, making music, telling stories, and having fun. The work was seasonal so we had to move several times per year, and while room and board and a small stipend were given, the pay wasn't anything one could live on sustainably. And there was no other role for me to grow into. After two years, with a heavy heart I realized it was time to move on.

My plan had been to move back to New York to become the next great Jewish drummer. Life intervened (not that my plan was any good). My mother's health was failing again. The liver they had given her wasn't working properly. She would need a second transplant. My grandmother had been taking care of her again, and after eight months together, they needed a break from each other. I felt called to go be with mom and help her through her transplant and send my grandmother home. After mom had the transplant, everyone thought she'd go back to work and so would I.

I drove to Florida to be with mom January of 2005. My grandmother went home. My mother was dangerously ill. She was in and out of the hospital for a few months. We stayed at a friend's beach house in Jacksonville, mom on the ground floor and I upstairs. When she was strong enough, we'd walk out on the beach, which she loved. She wasn't often strong enough. There were many days of fevers, chills, sweats, aches, and pains and I didn't know if she was going to make it. She'd say she was in so much pain she just wanted to die, and I had to try to reassure her. There were days when I came downstairs to check on her, and I honestly didn't know if I wanted her to still be alive. I begged God to either give her the transplant or take her already. It was agonizing to see her suffer.

On March 10th, we got the call that there was a liver for her. Rafi had come to visit for her birthday, the following day. The surgery did not go as planned. Mom's heart stopped twice during the surgery. She lost a lot of blood. She was incredibly swollen, so much so that they couldn't close the incision. A second trauma surgeon had to be called in to assist. After fourteen hours of surgery, she was brought to the intensive care unit, a trauma surgeon and a nurse watching over her all night. Rafi and I were told that the odds of her surviving the night were not good. We stood by her side and told her that if it was her time to go, she could but that we knew that if anyone could survive this it was her.

Mom stayed in intensive care for two months. Family and friends would visit for a few days when they could, but mostly I was alone taking care of her, walking the halls of the hospital, crying out to God and asking God to heal her. I had no community in Jacksonville. I knew one of the local rabbis, yet I wasn't at all interested in going to synagogue. What kind of God would allow this suffering to take place?

I had a few romantic encounters, and I started dating a non-Jewish woman. I'd never dated a non-Jew before – I was raised knowing that I'd marry a Jew, yet there were few Jewish singles I met in Jacksonville and none who I had any interest in. I started dating someone, though as I was spending all day in the hospital, high romance it wasn't. I told myself that one way or another I was going to leave Jacksonville, either with mom having gotten better or following her death. I thought it would be nice to have someone to talk to and be intimate with, and it was, though I was hardly in any condition to give much of my time or energy to her. In retrospect it was unfair of me to get involved with her, especially since I knew I could never marry her (let alone give her much attention). I felt especially terrible when she told me she started to have feelings for me and wanted me to meet her mother. Horrified at what I'd done, I told her I couldn't meet her mother and that she shouldn't feel deeply for me. She wisely broke it off. Sigh.

Two months after the transplant, mom woke up. Doctors didn't know why but she started showing signs of progress. They took her out of the induced coma she was in, and slowly but surely the swelling came down, and she started talking again. I was amazed. She was moved to a regular room in the hospital for a month, and then did a month of rehab, following which we drove home to New Jersey. It had been the longest eight months of my life. I was eager for her to get better so I could do something else. I was happy for her that she was getting better, yet at the same time I was pretty miserable. Food and pornography became my companions.

We returned to New Jersey, though unfortunately, she never got better enough to live on her own. The transplant gave her some time and she was starting to get acclimated again, but she was still in and out of the hospital. I stayed with her, managing her medications, her treatment, and whenever possible, her mood. She was not an easy patient. I felt trapped – I didn't want to stay but I couldn't leave her. We tried hiring caregivers a few times. They were often unskilled, didn't always speak English, didn't know her medications, and they were often out of shape. We were worried about mom falling – if they were so out of shape themselves how would they be able to pick mom off the floor? I had no choice but to stay.

I couldn't just be a caregiver, though. I was going stir-crazy and needed some intellectual stimulation. I stumbled across a work from home email and thought it was interesting. I invested in a real estate program, which I thought I might do from home. I had no business thinking of launching a real estate career then, though that training led me to the work of T. Harv Eker and Peak Potentials Training, a personal development company (now Success Resources America). I attended a few Peak Potentials seminars and loved the energy, the motivation, and the practical techniques to help us decide what we wanted in life and how to achieve it. I took Train the Trainer, their speaker training seminar, loved it, and signed up for the second one to be held in February 2007 a short drive from where we lived in New Jersey. I also did a two-year distance learning training to become a Maggid, an inspirational Jewish storyteller. In Eastern Europe there were many Maggidim who travelled from town to town, teaching Torah, and giving people hope and wisdom. My teacher Yitzhak Buxbaum had brought the art of the Maggidim back to life, and I loved his two-year training and was very proud to be ordained. I learned not just storytelling techniques, but I learned how to think differently about my own story, and how to use stories to help others grow and heal.

And yet, cancer returned. More treatments and hospital visits and wondering why mom wasn't getting better. I remember the call from the cancer specialist, which woke me up at six am in early February 2007. He told me the end was near. My grandmother and I rushed to the hospital. I knew it was my job to tell her the bad news. It turns out she already knew. I said "Mom, the doctors tell me you're not doing so well. They say you may not make it." She looked up at me and said "No shit." We got Shoshi and Rafi home from Israel, and Avi came as well. Mom spent the last few days of her life at the Robert Wood Johnson hospital in New Brunswick, surrounded by family and many friends. She was in her element, strong and talking, and she held on for Shoshi and Rafi to get home. On February 5th, when none of us were looking, she took her last breath.

Burying my mother was one of the hardest days of my life. I was still seeking her approval. I was still holding on to the idea that she might get better. I wanted her to live. I wanted to make her proud. I didn't want her to go, and I didn't know what to do with myself. We spent the week of shiva in New Jersey, after which I was left to clean up her apartment and her estate. But first, I had a decision to make. Train the Trainer 2 was happening just after shiva ended. Could I still go? I wasn't sure that I was emotionally able to be in an upbeat environment, yet the seminar was only held once a year and it was happening right where I lived. I remember sitting at the kitchen table and I felt my mother's presence telling me that I'd already put my life on hold for two years and that my not going to the seminar wasn't going to bring her back. I took her advice and went.

The seminar was life-changing. World-renowned speaker Les Brown spoke for two days. He chose three people to share a short inspirational message in front of the whole conference. I was chosen and received some feedback from Les over dinner. When it was my turn to talk, I shared about having been mom's caregiver and burying her the week before. The whole room was silent. I told people that when they're going through a crisis, hold on and keep going, ask for help, and appreciate every moment with their loved ones. As I shared my story, I felt a weight lift off my shoulders, and some of the burden I'd been carrying washed away in the tears I shed. Others told me that they needed to hear what I shared. I thanked Les for working with me, and I thanked Robert Riopel, the head trainer for choosing me. He told me he thought I could be a Peak Potentials trainer and lead their seminars someday. I was floored. Me? Leading seminars? Inspiring others? I had no idea that was possible, yet Robert gave me a bigger vision of myself.

I went home and spent several months cleaning out mom's estate. I was lonely and eating my way through my grief, and I started to think about what was next. I went back to City College to finish the last few classes I needed to graduate, and then debated between working for Peak Potentials and going to rabbinical school. I decided that I needed to become a rabbi, not for dad, but for myself. I wanted to learn how to bring spirituality, nature, music, song, and the best of Jewish wisdom together to unlock hearts and minds. I met Rabbi Zalman Schachter-Shalomi, leader of ALEPH, the Jewish Renewal movement, a progressive, mystical movement devoted to Jewish spirituality. Reb Zalman and ALEPH's approach to a joyful, heart-centered Jewish life amazed me. The light bulb went off again and I enrolled in the ALEPH Rabbinic program.

I moved to Boulder, Colorado where Reb Zalman lived, and was fortunate to study with him personally for a year, along with the ALEPH courses I participated in online and a few times per year at in-person retreats. I did trainings in prayer leadership, theology, spirituality, ritual storytelling, and sacred chant. I did a three-year training to become a Spiritual Director, helping to guide and heal others with better connections to God and themselves. I moved to Jerusalem to study for a year at Pardes, a center where many young Americans come to learn for a year (and one class at the Conservative Yeshiva, since I owed JTS one Talmud credit. It took me a while, but 13 years after I started college, I got the diploma!). I also became the drummer and rabbinic intern for Nava Tehila, a Jewish Renewal community known for musical, heartfelt, ecstatic prayer. Drumming with them was a major highlight of my year. When I was drumming amidst several hundred people, I could focus on the music and tune out my own existential doubt and anguish. Somehow when I drum, I can let go of the noise and focus on the holiness.

I had a few short relationships during rabbinical school. I was searching desperately for the person I was supposed to marry. Where was she and why didn't she show up already? I didn't find her in Israel. I moved to North Bergen, New Jersey to be the rabbi of a synagogue there. I had been there before on the High Holidays and they were in need of a young leader to try and rejuvenate an older congregation. I lived in a room in the back of the synagogue. There was a shower in the women's bathroom and a washer and dryer in the kitchen I could use. Luxurious living it wasn't, yet it gave me a place to call my own and a chance to step into my rabbinate for a few years. I had no social life though and didn't know what to do with myself when I wasn't leading services. The synagogue grew, yet on the inside I felt trapped. The leadership didn't seem willing to let me do what I felt was necessary, and I was spending my time mostly with people in their 70's and 80's.

They were lovely people, but there had to be more to life than that. I didn't have any local friends to connect with. I was frustrated, sad, angry, and I turned back to food, pornography, and watching endless hours of television. My life may have been a mess but at least on ER, Law and Order, and the West Wing things were being taken care of.

My rabbinical school classes kept me going. I loved the community and the learning was top-notch. I did a unit of Clinical Pastoral Education (CPE) at a hospital in New Jersey. I'd already spent more than my fair share of time in hospitals, so visiting patients wasn't hard for me. We had a month-long unit on addiction. I was struck by the reality that the questions the addicts in the videos were asking were the same questions I was asking. Am I an addict? What does that even mean? Jews can't be addicts, can they?

I went to an ALEPH event and met a fellow rabbinical student who seemed interesting. We had a nice conversation. Six months later, at another gathering, we connected again. She was very nice, funny, and kind. I invited her to come visit me at the synagogue and she did. We started dating. I was more than willing to make the two-hour drive to Philadelphia where she lived, and she'd come visit on weekends too. She seemed like the one!

She had studied about addiction, so I shared my questions with her. I was clear that I was an overeater. She was supportive, and introduced me to a functional medicine doctor who, after doing blood work and tests, told me I needed to eliminate flour, sugar, and dairy from my diet, eat a lot more vegetables, and start exercising regularly. Sigh. I went to a few recovery meetings about food. It was hard to give all that up. I had been so used to comforting myself with food. I'd go to the grocery store and tell myself I wasn't going to walk down certain aisles and I don't know how but those foods ended up in my cart. I gave up flour and sugar and started to exercise.

We got married December 2011, and I was ordained a few weeks later. I moved from North Bergen to Philadelphia for her last year of school. I didn't work much that year. I signed up for a life-coach certification training, excited to learn techniques to help others (and myself) grow. I worked as a freelance Jewish educator and consultant, and I did what I could to support my wife and give her all that I could. I was thrilled when she was ordained. Here we were two rabbis ready to make our mark on the world. We applied for jobs all over the Jewish world and were hired as co-rabbis of a 250-family Conservative synagogue in Memphis, Tennessee. We'd each work half-time, do some other work to supplement our income, and have a nice life together.

That was the plan, anyway. Things didn't quite turn out that way.

We didn't work well together. There was way too much to do, and we got there with a month to go before the High Holidays and we both had to meet everyone, prepare for the most important time in the Jewish year, get settled, and find time to connect with each other and continue building our young marriage. The job never stopped. The politics in the synagogue office were difficult. We had no clear delineation of who was doing what so even when we had meetings separately, we spent time each night recapping everything that was said. We both wanted to give so much to the congregation but struggled to figure out how to do so without stepping on each other's toes. We started to grow apart. I wondered what happened to the happiness we experienced when we were dating. How did we lose that? Could we find it again?

I suggested that we try couples counseling. The counselor helped me realize that I had helped create our dynamic, and I needed to take responsibility for when I shared my feelings and when I stayed silent, and how I shared my views. It takes two to tango and I needed to own my side of things and not blame my wife for everything I helped create. Our therapist suggested I go to a weeklong program called the Healing Trauma Program at Onsite, a healing center outside Nashville. I told no one from the synagogue I was going. After all, rabbis aren't supposed to have problems, and my parents always told me that if the congregation found out how messed up things were, Dad would be fired. I certainly didn't want to get fired for acknowledging my issues, and I hoped that my challenges, individually and within the marriage, could be resolved privately without the synagogue ever having to know that anything was wrong.

I had a life-changing week of healing. I learned at Onsite that children who grow up in dysfunctional homes have a higher tendency of addiction than those who grow up in happier homes. I learned that the more trauma you experience as a child, the more that trauma is going to take a toll. I learned that we all need healthy outlets to share our thoughts and feelings and I hadn't been giving myself permission to even have them for many years. I learned that I wasn't just addicted to food. I also had to deal with pornography, love addiction, codependency, skin-picking, hair-pulling, procrastination, perfectionism, shame, guilt, anger, grief, technology addiction, and more. I learned that I was carrying so much that I was smothering my emotions and not letting myself live. In a psycho-dramatic experience, I envisioned kicking my parents out of my head, telling them that I'd had enough with them controlling my thoughts, and showed them the door. That was empowering. (Obviously my mother was dead, and it was I who was keeping her negatively inside my head). I learned that there was a path forward if I committed to healing. I knew I needed to do it and that the time had come to make major changes. I suspected that the marriage was likely over, though I desperately wanted to be wrong about that. I thought the foundation of our marriage wasn't strong enough for us to survive. Sadly, I was right.

We weren't happy at work; we were even worse at home. I moved into the guest bedroom. I was miserable – yet again what I had thought was the relationship of my dreams was crumbling. I ate my emotions away, and my pornography use was rampant. I felt bad for using pornography while I was married. It felt a bit like I was cheating on her, and I hated that I was keeping secrets. I did eventually tell her about that, with my commitment to get help for my problems.

Still, I had learned good techniques at Onsite and I was committed to doing the work necessary to be happy. On December 19, 2014 I was visiting the used bookstore at Memphis's Central Library and perusing the books on addiction when a book caught my eye. Facing Love Addiction by Pia Melody. That book was the best two dollars and fifty cents I ever spent.

I took it home and read the first seventy pages that night, and the rest of it the following day. I didn't understand how Pia could describe me so clearly without ever having met me. Every symptom of love addiction she described was true for me. I understood that I had used pornography, and food, and my other addictions as ways to find connection, community, and healing. Originally, they had all been short-term ways of getting through difficult situations. Unfortunately, I stuck with them long past the point of their being useful.

I consider December 19, 2014 to be day one of my sobriety. A few weeks later I was at an ALEPH event and went to a recovery meeting there. I shared my woes and after the meeting one of the participants pulled me aside and said that he shared a lot of what I did and offered to be my sponsor. I didn't hesitate to say yes. I read a lot of recovery literature. I called my sponsor almost daily to check in. He was a lifeline I desperately needed.

I started attending a class called Codependency in Relationships at Hope Presbyterian Church in Memphis. For the first time, I began looking at the behaviors and patterns I brought to my relationships. My wife left during the summer of 2015. I was crushed yet determined to keep healing. I went to Hope Presbyterian's DivorceCare classes, which were all about divorce from a Christian perspective. I had to translate some of what the instructor said, yet it was good for me to be in a room with others going through divorce as well.

I went back to Peak Potentials and signed up for more of their programs. I started working with a life-coach twice a month to set goals for myself and think about who I could be if I stopped getting in my own way. I walked on hot coals, I swallowed fire, I did ropes courses,

and I went skydiving after the divorce was finalized. I started eating

better and going to the gym twice a week at the Jewish Community

Center in Memphis. I hired a trainer to keep me accountable, and my

health improved significantly. I joined Toastmasters and worked

through their speaking and leadership programs, becoming a

Distinguished Toastmaster, their highest level. I found a few great guys

to have lunch with regularly. We talked about healing, recovery,

spirituality and what a healthier approach to manhood could be.

I started participating in recovery meetings by phone, trying to

do one several times a week, and even once a day for a few months. I

listened to a lot of recovery podcasts. And yet, for a long time I refused

to go to a recovery meeting in Memphis. What if someone I knew saw

me there? Rabbis aren't supposed to have problems. When I got

divorced and shared about it on Facebook, some of my congregants

were horrified that I would share my emotions so publicly. There was

no way I was going to tell them of my addictions. I knew if I was found

out, I'd probably be fired. Still, my sponsor kept insisting that I needed

to go to meetings, and that the whole point of recovery is to find a

fellowship of people who are supporting each other's growth. That's

not possible nearly to the same extent with phone meetings. After much

persistence, I went back to Hope Presbyterian. They host a lot of meetings. There were two recovery meetings back to back I was interested in. I went to one of them, which was from a Christian perspective. I didn't know anyone there. Maybe this could work, I thought. When that meeting ended, I walked to the other side of the building to the second meeting. I was almost there when I hard from behind me "Hello, Rabbi". My heart sunk. Oh crap, I thought to myself. It's time to start packing. I turned around and said hello to someone who thankfully wasn't a member of my congregation. I didn't ask him where he was going, and he didn't ask me where I was going. We wished each other well, and I trusted that he would keep his mouth shut. Thankfully, he did. I went to the other meeting and kept going for the rest of my time in Memphis.

Slowly, I worked the steps with my sponsor. It took me a long time to wrap my head around the program. It was hard coming to grips with myself, with God, with my parents, and with everyone I needed to make amends to. Recovery is not easy. It takes a daily commitment to grow, to work on my issues, and to keep myself out of harm, each and every day, one day at a time.

I stayed on at the synagogue and became their full-time rabbi. Life at the synagogue got better, especially when my old friend Geo Poor became the Executive Director. My mind got better. My finances improved. Exercise was helping a lot. I talked to my sponsor at least

74

once a week. I talked to my coach twice a month. I talked to my spiritual director once a month. I hired a high-level coach who also specialized in addictions and he gave me suggestions as well. I started seeing a chiropractor once a month so he could realign my spine and a rib that tends to go out of alignment. I saw an NAET allergy healer who specializes in getting trauma out of one's system and I saw her weekly. Every time I processed my sadness and grief I felt better, yet there was always more to work through. I knew I had to keep going. Life was too short to hang on to the traumas and wounds of my past.

Through it all I didn't talk about the difficulties of my marriage at the synagogue. I had no need to disparage my ex-wife then or now and I'm grateful for the time we spent together. I wouldn't be who I am today without all that she taught me. I stayed at the synagogue without her and invested myself in the community. Still, after doing a lot of healing work I came to understand that I was bored in Memphis. While I did good work at the synagogue, I didn't really have friends. There was always too much work to do, and even on the rare occasions when I had time off to go listen to music, I realized I didn't have people to go listen to music with. The salary they were paying was entirely reasonable, and I could have stayed there except I knew there was more work for me to do in the world. I'm so grateful for my four years in Memphis. They gave me space to heal, and the opportunity to grow. I discovered Mussar, Jewish ethical literature. I went to a five-day

training for educators at Beit T'Shuvah, the Jewish recovery center in

Los Angeles, and I brought what I learned back to the synagogue. A

number of people in the community thanked me for bringing awareness

of addiction into the Jewish world. I realized that other than a small

number of books and Beit T'Shuvah I knew of no Jewish recovery

connections or programs. Why do most Jews have to go through

recovery without the support of the Jewish community? Why are most

recovery meetings in churches instead of synagogues hosting their

own? Why aren't there online forums for Jews in recovery to connect?

Why don't we talk more about addiction in the Jewish world? And why

can't rabbis have space to talk about their own issues without fear of

being fired? I wondered about all of this and more.

In the summer of 2016, on Tu B'Av, also known as Jewish

Valentine's Day, I posted a message on Facebook that I was ready to

start dating again. I had done a lot of work with my brain trust of

sponsor, coaches, spiritual director, recovery friends, and healers

(sometimes it feels like it takes a whole team to keep my head on

straight!). I received a few messages and had conversations with a few

different people. My friend Nechama, who I had studied with at Pardes,

told me a friend of hers was also looking and wondered if she might

connect us. As it turns out, her friend Sherri had also posted on

Facebook a month before I did that she was looking, and because Sherri and I had both lived in DC in 2004, I knew her and had seen her Facebook post. As it turns out, she had also seen mine, yet we were both too shy to reach out. Thanks to Nechama, we connected and started talking on Facebook messenger. We kept talking as the other possibilities all whittled away. We slowly built up to talking on the phone and on video chat. We were long-distance between Memphis and Silver Spring, and it was only after three months that we had our first date in person. I had come up for Rafi's wedding, and decided to spend a few extra days with Sherri to see if we had what to talk about in person. We certainly did and decided to see where this could lead. We were long-distance for a year, flying back and forth every few weeks to spend time together. I worked with my brain trust to set healthy expectations and make sure I wasn't jumping head over heels like I had at the beginning of every other relationship. I wondered if she was normal, and if there were warning signs I was missing. I couldn't find any (other than the fact that she liked me).

After a few months I knew I needed to tell Sherri about my addiction and recovery. I suspected we were headed towards marriage – I certainly hoped so – and it wasn't fair to keep it from her. She visited for New Years and on Saturday afternoon after services we had a very long conversation about all of it. I was worried she might be scared and run away. She listened to everything I shared, looked at me and said, "I'm still here." As a social worker Sherri understands trauma and healing. And she knows that people in recovery can live wonderful lives so long as they keep working the program. She said she had no reason to go anywhere. My heart soared when she said that. I told her I loved her. She loved me as well.

A few months later, we went ring shopping and in June, I proposed. The idea of spending my life together with Sherri was one that made me incredibly happy. I planned to finish up my time at the synagogue, move to Silver Spring, and take some time to get married, get settled, launch the Jewish motivational podcast I'd been thinking about, finish the coaching certification, and become a freelance rabbi, coach, storyteller, and drummer.

I moved to Silver Spring August 1st, launched the Torah of Life podcast September 20th (my birthday), and we got married October 22, 2017. I've started teaching about Judaism and addiction and recovery, and have been blessed to make music with Nava Tehila, be a guest rabbi in a few different congregations, and begin finding opportunities in the greater Washington, DC area.

Life had another curveball for me though. The week after our wedding, Dad ended up in the hospital with shortness of breadth. After many tests, he was eventually diagnosed with lung cancer. The doctors originally thought it was stage one or two and treatable, though it was eventually determined to be stage four. Sigh. He was holding his own for a few months, and then in and out of the hospital in the beginning of 2018. I completed a coaching certification training in February and was all set to launch my coaching practice. A day or two after I returned, I heard from the doctors that dad's cancer was not going to get better, and he only had two months at most to live. I flew down to Florida and spent much of March and April with him and Ellen, his wife. He was a rabbi and a grief specialist, and he and I shared a special bond, and would consult each other around congregational dynamics, sermons, music, and our shared love of professional wrestling. Dad died April 22nd, and we buried him a few days later.

How do I know recovery works, my friends?

When Mom died, I cried and I ate a lot of my feelings. When other tragedies struck, I turned to overeating, pornography, skin-picking, hair-pulling, television, gaming, and overwork. When Dad died, I had said all that I needed to say to him beforehand. It hurt a lot when he died. It still does. And yet instead of processing my grief and sadness in unhealthy ways I share my feelings with friends. I go to meetings. I call my sponsor. I listen to inspirational podcasts. I talk to my wife. I go for a walk or listen to music. I don't act out. That's how I know recovery works. Dad died, and I'm okay. I miss him, and I love him, and I'm okay, which is exactly what he would want.

Today, I'm glad to say that my journey of recovery has opened my eyes to who I can be when I work a recovery program and when I refuse to settle for less than a great life. I'm not going to tell you that my life is perfect. Far from it. I'm not going to tell you that I don't ever think about the foods I no longer eat, or the pornography I no longer watch. I have good days, and I have bad days. I'm a work in progress, just like you. All I can say is that by the grace of God and the fellowship of recovery, I am happy, joyous, and free, one day at a time, and I'll do everything I can to keep it that way and to help others get that way for the rest of my life.

I don't know exactly what the future holds. I hope that this book will help jumpstart the Our Jewish Recovery movement, and that the Jewish world will learn to embrace those who are suffering. I want to see Serenity Shabbats in every Jewish city once or twice a year, a Jewish recovery podcast, cruises, books, webinars, retreats, online learning experiences and community. I'd love to have your involvement. Together, we can make this happen.

I pray that this book helps you on your journey of recovery and healing and offers you a path forward to a healthier and better life. If I can get and stay sober, so can you. I hope you'll use the strategies and teachings in this book to give you strength while you're working your program of recovery. I'd love to hear your reflections and I'd be happy to be a resource and share other learning with you. Don't hesitate to be in touch with me at rabbiilan@torahoflife.com. Thank you again for reading this book and for sharing your story and wisdom.

A better life awaits all of us, if we dare to claim it. Are you ready to write a new chapter to your story? Turn the page, and let's begin.

Are You Ready
for a New Beginning?

Step 1 – We admitted we were powerless over our addiction,

that our lives had become unmanageable.

The first thing David said to me was "my life is messed up. I can't go on like this anymore. I don't know what else to do." David had been in a car accident a year before. After several surgeries, he became addicted to his pain meds. Doctors wouldn't give him any more so he bought them on the street. He spent his savings on drugs and started drinking again as well. His home life was in shambles. His job fired him for stealing. He hadn't had a proper meal with his wife and kids in months. He didn't even know how to look them in the eye anymore. He felt like a failure every time he saw them. He used to be able to provide for them, spend time with them. Now, he was spending money they didn't have just to find relief from his pain. He felt he was losing his family in the process. It wasn't hard to see why. The only place he thought he could win was at the casino. Sometimes he won enough to tide him over. If he could just get a few lucky breaks, and find a new job, he thought he could turn everything around, have enough money for pills, be a better father and husband, and save his family.

David's challenges were overwhelming. He was trying desperately to convince himself he could make it on his own, and only occasionally admitting he was in over his head. He saw his purpose and identity as a provider for his wife and children. Now he was unable to do so and saw himself as a failure. David needed help, as quickly as possible. We talked for hours, and he said he was willing to think about getting help. I gave him some phone numbers to call when he was ready, and we made an appointment for the following week, though I told him I'd make time for him sooner if he was willing. I saw him again, yet he never continued the conversation. He made it clear he didn't want my help. I told him that was fine, though if he ever changed his mind, I'd be more than willing to assist. I hope that someday he allows himself the gift of recovery and support.

The hardest thing we can ever do is to admit that we need help, that life as we know it isn't working. Like David, we tell ourselves we can keep holding it together, that all can be well if we just hold on; somehow, we will make it through. It's not actually that bad, we say, look at all the people who have it worse than we do. We don't actually have anything to complain about. There are people much poorer than me, what right do I have to complain?

Shira told me the same thing when I met her for coffee. She said she couldn't tell anyone in her religious circles that she was struggling to keep up with the constant demands of her children, their day school, synagogue, and community life. Her husband worked 60-70 hours each week and was always running off to volunteer and pray at the synagogue. She felt alone and abandoned, and she was tired of putting on a false front. She was exhausted and the only time she felt solace was when the kids were asleep, and she could sit and drink. It was only supposed to be one glass every now and then, but now she told me it was up to three or four, several nights a week. She felt better when she drank, but she knew this couldn't be healthy. She was hiding bottles from her husband and had to make up quick excuses when their daughter found one. She didn't want to let go of the one thing she relied on, and she had no one she could talk to about this. She sought me out and asked what to do. She felt guilty for even asking. "I have a roof over my head, children who love me, and a husband who pays the bills. So many others have it worse, and this is the life I signed up for. I shouldn't complain, I'm just not sure how much longer I can live like this."

Shira had that nagging feeling we get in the pit of our stomachs, which doesn't go away just because we want it to. She was afraid to make the necessary changes to her life and didn't want to hurt the ones she loved. It was easier to just keep drinking; she'd only be hurting herself, she thought. Of course, the more she drank, the less she recognized herself as the mother she wanted to be for her children. I worked with Shira to help her understand that she needed help, and that she and her family deserved better. It took a long time to get her to accept that she was worthy of being helped. Her parents had both worked long hours, and she was raised to place their needs, and those of her younger siblings, over her own. At her urging, I was present when she told her husband about the drinking. He had suspected something was off but was shocked to hear the news. He was also struggling to keep up with his job and the synagogue and agreed to manage his time better, give up some volunteer roles, and spend more time with Shira and the children. Shira got into an outpatient recovery program and hasn't had a drink for the last few years. She and her husband worked with me to create a lifestyle they could both fully embrace. They rekindled their romance and are happier than ever. It took a lot of work to rebuild their marriage on a better foundation, and they both agree it was worth it.

Their story only improved because they were both willing to be honest and vulnerable with each other. They recognized that if they didn't make changes, their marriage would likely fall apart. I encouraged them to be completely honest with each other about all that they were thinking and feeling. Thankfully, they did, and I'm glad that they are doing well today.

Unfortunately, the secrets we've kept buried don't go away. "You're only as sick as your secrets," we're told in recovery meetings. The feelings we've been running from for far too long don't go away. The consequences of our choices are harder and harder to ignore. Arrest and imprisonment. Alienation from friends and family. Financial struggles. Poor health. Sadness and depression. Shame and guilt. I'm not good enough. I'm not smart enough. Why am I a mess? Can my life ever get better?

We drown ourselves in our sorrows. No one wants to hear what I have to say. I can't stop what I'm doing, I'll let everyone else down. I don't have time to get help. I don't even know that I'm worth helping. Maybe I really am worthless and unlovable after all. If I were smarter, I wouldn't have gotten myself into this mess in the first place – I deserve my sorry lot in life.

I spent years telling myself that I wasn't good enough, smart enough, kind enough, handsome enough to have what I wanted. I suspect you have as well. None of it was true, but I clung to those justifications. **What story are you telling yourself that might not serve you any longer? What secrets are you carrying and how are they harming you?**

86

Tony Robbins says, "it is in our moments of decision that our destiny is shaped". For too long we have made a decision to stay comfortable with our pain and suffering. Deep down, we blame ourselves for our misery. We deserve it. It's our fault, and we'll never be happy, we'll never have peace.

I thought I was only valuable when I was helping others, and I spent as much time as I could doing so. I tried everything I could to not be alone with my thoughts, eating and fantasizing my feelings away. Someone else will save me. Something else will make me feel better. **Who are you looking to, to save you from yourself?** If it hasn't worked yet, what makes you think it will in the future? Maybe it's time for you to let others help you move forward. There is no magic bullet, no magical cure for the wounds of the soul. Nothing else and no one else can do the inner work I refused for so long to do. Are you willing to reach out to others who've shared your struggles and let them help you? Can you find it inside you to begin again?

Albert Einstein said, "we cannot solve our problems with the same thinking we used when we created them". We have been fighting reality, refusing to change course for far too long. It has cost us friendships, relationships, jobs, money, sanity, health, stability, freedom, and so much more. I can hold on; I haven't hit rock bottom yet. Just another day, and then I'll get help. Maybe tomorrow, just not now.

It's terrifying to think that our lives will never get better. On the other hand, if you've spent years thinking that you're miserable, worthless, and deserve every punishment that comes your way, you might not want to accept help when it's offered. Happiness gets in the way of misery. **Is it possible that you've held on to your suffering a little too long?** Is it possible that if millions of others can turn their lives around and get clean and sober, maybe you can as well?

Today is as good a day as any to begin anew.

Are you ready to try again, my friend?

I invite you to think of all of the pain in your life that comes from not accepting that life could be better. What are the consequences of not surrendering to the reality that you might need help? What pain has your addiction caused? Feel that pain deeply. You have held on to this pain for far too long. What would life look like without it? Can you even imagine a different future? You may not be able to. I don't think I could when I started. **Sometimes you have to believe in other people's belief in you just to get through.** I needed my sponsor and recovery friends to believe that I could make it. If you're reading this book, and willing to do the work, **I believe you can make it. You're strong enough, and if I can do it, so can you.**

If you are ready to take a step in the direction of your better future, my first recommendation is to go find a recovery meeting near you, listen to stories of others who have benefited from recovery, and ask for their help. Find someone you resonate with and ask if they'll sponsor you. It may take you some time to find the right meeting or the right sponsor. You may need medical help, counseling, or rehab. You won't find all of the solutions right from the start – go to meetings, take care of your medical and spiritual needs, ask what others do to get better, and follow their advice. The mishna says "לֹא הַבַּיְשָׁן לָמֵד - a person prone to being ashamed can not learn."[37] Don't be shy about asking for help (but make sure you're asking the right people for help. Your drinking buddy won't help you get sober. Your new friends in the meetings will.)

Along with meetings, I encourage you to find time to be with yourself every day, even for just a few minutes. As you begin your recovery journey, I recommend you find a quiet space, journal your answers to these questions, and get clear on where your life has taken you. Place your hand on your heart, breathe deeply and feel how much sadness you carry within you. Tell yourself out loud that your life isn't working and admit it to yourself fully. Let the tears flow. **You don't have to live from this place of desperation anymore. You are**

worthy of love, and you can find community and a new way forward.

From this day forward, resolve to do all that you can to begin anew. One teacher of mine taught us a phrase coined by Emile Coue, a French psychologist and pharmacist and I encourage you to say it each morning and evening: **"every day, in every way, I am getting better and better."**[38] Affirmations can help you talk more positively to yourself. Feel free to create your own affirmations. A few suggestions to try: You resolve to heal your pain, and to bring more peace into your life. You may not know where the road ahead will lead, but you commit to finding people who can help free you from all the ways in which you don't yet practice self-love. You commit to asking for help, and not stopping until you get it. From this day forward, you'll try to do all that you can to see yourself as a valuable, holy, creative, worthy member of the human race, entitled to a life of blessings and service. From this day forward, you'll choose to open your heart to love. **From this day forward, you choose life!**

Feel the energy of this new decision. Embrace it. Breathe it in and let it fill you. You are setting out on a brave journey of healing and transformation. It won't be easy and there will be challenges, yet new friends will emerge, and angels you may not even know will escort you every step of the way. You are brave enough and strong enough to find recovery, one day at a time. I honor your choice, and I believe a better future is possible. **With God's help and with the support of family and friends and the recovery community, you can make it through. It works if you work it, one day at a time.**

Here I Am, God: Hineni

Step 2 – Came to believe that a Power greater than ourselves

could restore us to sanity

Step 3 – Made a decision to turn our will and our lives

over to the care of God as we understood God

Once we surrender living according to our own ego, we need a new operating system. When we decide that our ego can no longer be the master we serve, we must find a new way of thinking, of living, and of being.

Many addicts (and many non-addicts) have a hard time with the idea of God. If God is all-powerful, why do bad things happen? If God is all knowing, does God not care about me? Theologians and philosophers have debated these questions for thousands of years. For our purposes, **your job is to discover the God or belief system you can believe in and place your trust there.** What were you taught about God as a child? What did you learn from your parents, your clergy, and your teachers? Do those ideas and beliefs still work for you? What kind of God can you believe in? If even the idea of God doesn't work for you, can you place your trust in love, in the group or recovery fellowship, and/or in the goodness of humanity? Find something that you can rely on and see how it feels. Nothing you decide now is permanent – our approach to finding God can and ought to change over the years as we grow. Try on a metaphor and see how it fits. You may need to update your God-map every now and then to keep it fresh.

I believe in a God who helps bring us out of the slavery of our addictions and into the freedom of sobriety, serenity, and a life of meaning, each and every day. I don't believe that God is responsible for every bad thing that happens in the world – God doesn't cause car accidents, God doesn't give you cancer or illness, God doesn't cause war, famine, violence, and environmental degradation – humans are responsible for those, and humans can solve them. God is always here, sending us love and support, crying with us when we're sad, and celebrating with us when we're happy. God always has my best interest at heart, and God works God's magic in ways I often can't understand until later, if ever. I can always turn to God for support, whether to cry out in pain, to sing and dance in joy, and every emotion in-between. That's the God I have come to believe in.

You may have a different approach to God and that's entirely acceptable. Rabbi Zalman Schachter-Shalomi used to say "the God you don't believe in, I also don't believe in." Can you imagine a God that

cares about your wellbeing? Can you imagine a God who loves you

unconditionally? Take some time to think deeply about what kind of

relationship you want with God. What would you like from God, and

what can you give God in return? What name should you call God?

Sovereign? King? Source of the Universe? If you could have a

conversation with God, what would you say and how would you

imagine God responding? You don't have to have the answers to these

questions now. These are suggestions to help get you started.

When Rabbi Nachman of Bratzlav started devoting his life to

God as a young boy,

> "everything he did required great toil and effort. No form of
> devotion came easily, and the Rebbe literally had to lay down his life in
> many cases. Each thing required tremendous effort, and he had to work
> hard each time he wanted to do something to serve God. He fell a
> thousand times, but each time he picked himself up and served God
> anew...The Rebbe became accustomed to constantly beginning anew.
> Whenever he fell from his particular level, he did not give up. He
> would simply say 'I will begin anew. I will act as if I am just beginning
> to devote myself to God and this is the very first time'...Draw yourself
> to God with all your might. Remain strong, no matter how low you
> fall...Whether you go up or down, always yearn to come close to God.
> You may be brought low, but cry out to God, and do everything you
> can to serve Him in joy.'"[39]

Moses, our greatest prophet, was described as a servant of God.

The Mishna states "בְּכָל דְּרָכֶיךָ דָעֵהוּ" - in all your ways, know God".[40]

What does it mean to trust in God? Alan Morinis, founder of the

Mussar Institute, writes:

94

"Bitachon (trust) comes in two forms. There is the trust that God will look out for you. This is the trust that says God will deliver the providence you want and need....Rabbi Yosef Yozel Hurwitz, the Alter of Novarodok, understood bitachon this way. He wrote: 'The man of bitachon can turn away from all of life's problems for he knows that he will not want. What he must provide for, the needs of the body, he does in peace and contentment for he knows that no one can take away what the Creator allotted to him. In times of danger, he does not tremble. He walks securely and does not fear for tomorrow, for as long as he relies on the Almighty, he has everything'....

...There is another more reasonable, less radical version of trust based on an attitude of acceptance. You don't expect that everything will turn out as you want, but instead accept whatever happens because you understand that there is reason and order behind the world – that nothing takes place without a reason, even if the reason is not apparent to you at the moment. So you still don't worry whether you'll get food tomorrow, not because you feel assured that food will come, but because you accept whatever lies in store for you."[41]

Accepting what comes our way is not easy. Years ago, I interviewed to become the Chief Programming Officer of a new Jewish Community Center being built in New Jersey. I was a finalist and was excited by the idea of the job and all that I could do in it. I was devastated when I wasn't selected. I yelled at God – why God, have you abandoned me? I'm a good person, I teach Torah, isn't getting the job I want a good thing? Why don't you love me?

I ended up moving to Memphis, and had four powerful years of learning, growth, and recovery. Shortly after I arrived in Memphis, my sister sent me a newspaper article, which said that with six weeks left in construction of the $16-million building, they ran out of money and had to sell it to another organization. Had I been hired for the job; I would quickly have been out of a job! Maybe God was watching out for me after all. When I heard the news, I thanked God for sending me to Memphis, and I apologized to God for my getting angry unnecessarily. I understood that things aren't always as they seem – **sometimes God works miracles for us even when we can't see them.**

Look back over your own life. Can you see ways where perhaps there was a disappointment in your life that turned out to be a blessing? Were there times when God may have been supporting you, bringing angels and opportunities into your life that you couldn't then see? Make a list of those times. What have been the blessings in your life? What has given you courage and strength during the difficult times? Einstein said "coincidences are God's way of remaining anonymous." Is it possible that God has been your silent partner all along?

The dictionary defines sanity as "the ability to think and behave in a normal and rational manner." "Soundness or health of mind." "The state of not being mentally ill." Are you willing to try out the proposition that belief in God can help you find more sanity in the world? Are you willing to accept the idea that God can do for you what you can't do for yourself? If you can't, can you at least believe in the power of your recovery fellowship, and/or in the power of love?

If you're ready to accept that idea, I invite you to stand up, place your hand on your heart, breathe deeply, and talk to God. Words from your heart are always welcome in your prayers to God. If you'd like a suggestion, you might say God, I know I haven't always felt connected to you. I've been angry at you, I've shouted at you, I've doubted your very existence, and I've refused to let you into my life. I'm sorry about all of that, God. I see now that you've been by my side, and I'm grateful for all the blessings you've sent my way, the ones I know about, and the ones I can't possibly see. God, I hereby decide to let you into my life again. I will try to reach out to you more, to listen for the still small voice of your guidance, and I invite you to help me as I try each day to turn my life around. I know you are listening, and I appreciate any wisdom and support you can send my way, in whatever time and place it makes sense to do so. Thank you for the blessings of my life. Hineni – here I am, please use me as You see fit, and help me do Your will in the world. I ask only for the strength and the wisdom to do Your will, as best I can.

Though I walk through the valleys of life, and though I don't even know the way forward, I place myself in Your care.

"I yield my soul unto Your hand, at night, asleep,

and when I rise. For as long as I have breath,

You are with me; I shall not fear."[42]

Lay Your Wounds Bare

Step 4 - Made a searching and fearless moral inventory of ourselves

Step 5 – Admitted to God, to ourselves, and to another human being the exact nature of our wrongs

Congratulations, you've made it through the first three steps of the program. That takes courage. **Now, it's time to clean up your life, address your emotional self, and get to know who you really are.** I've met many people who say that step four is the hardest step, since it requires taking a real honest look at yourself and seeing where you need improvement.

That said, I want to encourage you to **also take a look at the good parts of your life.** Even though we tend to be hard on ourselves, there are certainly things we do well, and it's important to identify those too, lest we buy into our own negative self-talk. I'm sure that there are things about your life you can be proud of. Knowing what they are will help you going forward.

Rebbe Nachman said:

"Know that we have to judge everyone from a compassionate perspective. Even in someone who is completely evil, we have to search and find some little good thing. By this means—i.e. finding some little good thing, and judging compassionately—we truly raise the person up in compassion, and we are able to bring him back in teshuvah...Similarly, each of us must find [good] also in ourselves... we must seek and find some bit of good in us—for how is it possible that in all our days, we haven't done some mitzvah? It is impossible that there is no slight bit of good in the mitzvah and sacred deed...and we have to find it in order to revitalize ourselves and to achieve joy."[43]

How do we do this work of cheshbon hanefesh, accounting of the soul? Here are a few suggestions. First, have a look at the VIA Institute of Character's twenty-four-character traits, read the description of each trait, and then journal about how each trait appears in your life, both positively and negatively. You can take their free diagnostic test, which will help you set a baseline to work off of.[44]

The Mussar world has identified middot, character traits, and you can study them and also think about how they manifest in your life, both positively and negatively. There are a number of middot classification systems. Rabbi Israel Salanter, founder of the Mussar movement identified thirteen key character traits: truth, alacrity, diligence, honor, tranquility, gentleness, cleanliness, patience, order, humility, justice, thrift, and silence. You can find many descriptions of those thirteen character traits online, and in Mussar literature.[45] Rabbi Menachem Mendel of Satanov focused on thirteen middot as well: equanimity, patience, order, decisiveness, cleanliness, humility, righteousness, frugality, diligence, silence, calmness, truth, and separation.[46] Some say there are forty-eight middot.[47] Interestingly enough, the middot were influenced by Benjamin Franklin, and you can see how the Mussar leaders incorporated his work.[48] You can also take a look at the High Holiday liturgy, which include the Ashamnu and Al Chet prayers, which list all sorts of sins we may have participated in. How many of them apply to you?[49]

Talk with your sponsor, coach, and recovery friends to see what they recommend. I would also take time to go over your list with people who know you well. It's always good to get honest feedback from others. It's not easy hearing about our shortcomings, and it's also important to remember that **everyone has shortcomings. We all make mistakes, that's part of being human.** There's no need to beat yourself up over it – something tells me you've probably been doing that long enough.

Every day is an opportunity for us to do teshuvah, the work of repentance. In fact, our sages say that we should repent one day before we die. How do we know when we'll die? We don't, therefore we should do teshuvah every day to make sure we leave this world with a clean slate.[50]

When I was in high school, I was learning how to drive in my family's Chevy Astro minivan. It was a big box of a van, with eight seats. Because I have a lazy eye, it took me some time to figure out where in the road I should be looking. Shortly after getting my learner's permit, my grandparents came to visit us for Passover. When it was time for them to go home again, my mother was supposed to drive but wasn't feeling well that day, and dad was at work. It was decided that I would drive the van, with my grandfather sitting in the front passenger seat next to me, and my mother and grandmother in the row behind us.

We lived in Fairfax, Virginia at the time, which meant taking my grandparents to the airport on the beltway, in a big minivan, with only a learner's permit, and a lazy eye. I didn't have a choice, so off we went. When we got on the beltway, I struggled to make sure I was in the lane. I literally pressed my body against the window so that I could see where the lines on the left side of the lane were, so that I could avoid crossing over into the next lane. My mother and grandmother were screaming from the back seat, saying I was too close to the bus, the truck, and the other cars. I yelled back at them that yelling at me wasn't helpful (my yelling at them to stop yelling at me wasn't either). My grandfather then did something I'll never forget. He placed one hand out in front of him, and if I veered too far to the left, he moved his hand a bit to the right. When I moved too far to the right, he moved his hand to the left. I followed his lead the rest of the way to the airport, and everyone calmed down.

When I think of teshuvah, of repentance, I picture my grandfather with his hand in front of him. **Sometimes, we stray too far to the right, or too far to the left, and our job is just to move ourselves back to the center,** so we can keep driving, and keep living in the middle of our lanes. The thing is, **life is a journey of course-correction.** Flights are off-course ninety-percent of the time, and pilots are constantly course-correcting[51]. The same is true for us. We need not judge ourselves harshly – it's a natural part of the human condition. Like my grandfather's instructions, we can just move ourselves back to where we're supposed to be.

After you've worked through your character traits and defects, it's time to share them with God, with yourself, and with your sponsor. Why isn't it enough just to write them down? For starters, if you don't share them you won't have someone else to hear you, to guide you, to offer feedback and support. Working through your character defects will undoubtedly stir up issues for you – it's designed to do so. It is crucial to have support while you're doing this. Otherwise you'll be too tempted to give up and go back to your addiction. This is hard work, and I know you can do it. **Don't stop before the miracle happens.**

Your sponsor, coach, recovery friends, and/or loved ones can also tell you when you're being too hard on yourself, and when you're not being quite hard enough. I remember going through all of these traits and while there were things, I appreciated about myself, it felt incredibly overwhelming to list all the ways in which I was a less-than-perfect human. Interestingly enough, getting me to realize my imperfections was a big step. Sometimes we think we're perfect, and God's greatest gift to mankind. We're not. It was said of Rabbi Simcha Bunim of Pshischa that he used to carry two pieces of paper, one in each pocket. The first said "For my sake was the world created." The second said "I am but dust and ashes."[52] You might choose to have those pieces of paper in your pockets as well, or thankfully today you can order a coin online. Regardless, our goal is to remember that neither statement is true. They are each other's antidotes, yet neither is accurate. **We're not nothing, and we're not the most important something either. We have mediocrity inside us, and we have greatness inside us, and everything in between.**

When you share your character defects with your sponsor, coach, clergy, or therapist, you will be heard, perhaps for the first time in your life. They are not there to judge you, but to guide you along the program and help you live well. When I shared my 4th step with my sponsor, I knew that he wasn't going to judge me, he was going to hear me, and ask me clarifying questions, so that I could understand who I really was. You will need to be vulnerable in sharing with your sponsor. When it feels hard, remember your goal of getting through the steps and healing your life. Also remember what researcher Brene Brown teaches, that **"vulnerability is the core of fear, but also the birthplace of love and belonging"**.[53]

When you name your shame, you will find that its power lessens over you. When you get clear on all the ways you've been living poorly, you can set new habits to ensure a better future. I urge you to be kind to yourself while going through this process. This is not easy work, and you're doing it.

It's important to admit our defects to another human being, to ourselves, and to God. These are three different conversations. Your sponsor will tell you which conversation to have first. I recommend starting with your sponsor or coach, so that it gets out of your head and you get some positive feedback. Then you can stand in front of a mirror and have the conversation with yourself. Read slowly and make eye contact with yourself, taking it in. Finally, have a good conversation with God and acknowledge that you have work to do, and ask for help to continue on your healing journey. When I talked to God I did so in front of the ark in the synagogue I worked at. It was very peaceful, and very moving to feel that God heard me. You don't have to have the conversation in synagogue (though it's a great place to do so) – you can talk to God in nature, and in any quiet space. The important thing is to have the conversation, and to remind yourself that you're doing so for the purpose of healing, bringing God more into your life, and setting out on a new direction.

Are you ready to do it? Go for it. You've got nothing to lose except your pride, and we can all benefit from increased dosages of humility. I believe that God will be there listening to you, supporting you, and nourished by your bravery and your open-heartedness and vulnerability. You've come a long way, and I'm proud of you. I hope you are as well. Keep going, and make sure you tell God, your sponsor, and yourself everything. Don't keep any secrets. Identify all your strengths and weaknesses, share them, and then ask yourself:

What do I need to do to be better?

Who do I want to be?

What character traits would I like to have?

Now is a great time for you to think about who you want to grow into. Are there 3-5 traits you want to work on this year? Find a mussar group to study them in depth. Watch TED talks and read books on the subject. **We are always in a process of becoming** – may you be blessed with the strength to become your very best self each and every day, one day at a time.

Let Go And Let God

*Step 6: Were entirely ready to have God remove
all these defects of character.*

"Rabbi Ya'acov Yosef of Polnoye…taught that 'in every pain there is a holy spark from God, but it is concealed with many garments. When a person focuses on the fact that God is present even in the pain, the garment is removed, and the pain vanishes.'"[54]

Now it's time for another big step on your recovery journey, asking God to remove all the defects of character you identified in step four. It sounds simple, and yet, this too is not an easy step, for **it takes great courage to admit we need God's help in laying down what we've carried for so long.** Are you ready to accept help? You might be struggling with this idea and have a few questions, such as:

Am I ready to let go of my resentments, my fears, my pain, and my defects of character? Am I still attached to being the wounded, lonely, resentful, angry, and sad version of myself, desperately trying to be heard, seen, and loved in the world?

Of course, I'm ready – how could I not be ready to live a better, happier, more recovered life? And yet, the doubts remain.

I have carried my angst for decades. I have schlepped my tsuris, my pain and suffering with me for as long as I can remember.

Who will I be if I let go of my baggage? Will I still be me or will I become a figment of my former self? Will I be left with a gaping hole if the person I know disappears? Who will I become?

I am afraid of the unknown future. I don't know who I can be without my sufferings. And yet, I know that I need to become that which You want me to be. I know that I have come too far to turn around. I don't know who I am to be without my defects of character.

I only know that I am ready for You to remove them from me – all of them – even the ones part of me wants to desperately cling to since I've known them for so long and can't imagine being without them.

Only with Your help can I move forward and continue to grow and heal. I know I have resisted, I have bargained, I have cajoled, I have complained. Now with as much strength as I can muster, I officially declare:

I am ready to get out of Your way. I am ready to do Your will, not mine. Hineni. Here I am.

I recommend you bring this, and anything you wish to add, with you to a mikvah, a Jewish ritual bath, though a mountaintop or quiet natural setting also works. Step seven is often done together with step six, so feel free to prepare that now as well. Traditionally used by people converting into Judaism and as an opportunity for women's rebirth after each menstrual cycle, the mikvah has been reclaimed by many as a vehicle for our own healing. There is something powerful about having a conversation with God, while standing alone in a pool of water. If you wish, you can ask your sponsor, coach, rabbi, or a close friend to come with you.

I believe that **when we open our hearts to talk to God, God always listens**. God desires the open heart of mankind. "The candle of God is the soul of man, searching the inner chambers."[55] We are searching the world looking for God, and at the same time we are searching our own chambers, looking to remove our defects, our fears, and our pain, asking God to fill us instead with the light of holiness.

Step 7: Humbly asked God to remove our shortcomings.

Now you have a chance to offer your own prayers to God, asking for God to take away all that you don't want to carry anymore. You may wonder how that can be possible. So did I. I'll be honest – I don't think God removes our shortcomings in an instant. I think when we invite God to guide us, we have a moment of release and in that moment a shift can take place inside us. When we let God in, we can relax, and from a more relaxed state we can begin to make better decisions going forward. The doubts will return – we are invited to turn to God for assistance each time they do. I think **God needs our help to remove our shortcomings – if we turn to God on a regular basis and work a program of recovery, we will find that our character changes and we become better people.** That process doesn't happen overnight, yet overnight we can make major progress, with God by our side.

So, turn to God once again – from within a mikvah or in another quiet space. Ask God for your pain and sorrow and all your shortcomings to be lifted, and for all that your heart desires. (You might also ask God to direct your desires, so that you only want that which is good for you).

Don't be shy about pouring your heart out to God in this moment. You will feel better if you say everything. The secrets you've carried God already knows, yet it will do you good to share them. You can write your intentions or bring the following with you. Make sure that you say everything you need, and feel free to repeat this step as necessary. If you need a suggestion for what to say, feel free to use these words I wrote when I was preparing for this step.

Ribono Shel Olam, Master of the World, it is Your will for me, not mine, that I wish to achieve. You've given me glimpses of the person I believe You wish me to become.

I have done my best to follow Your direction, and yet, I have also distracted myself. I have run away. I have refused. I have ignored You. I have blamed You for problems I have created, and problems, which I learned and/or inherited, which I have perpetuated.

I have kept anger and insecurity, fear, pride, resentment, and doubt as my companions. I have taken guidance from them, and not nearly enough from You.

Holy One of Blessing, I ask You to remove my defects and my shortcomings. I appreciate that I picked up each of them as a strategy to keep me safe, and many of them did in the past. However, they keep me from being my best self, and they keep me from hearing and heeding Your call.

I give myself over to Your care. I know not how You operate, yet I know that You have taken these defects of characters from others, and I ask that You now do the same with me. Help me lay them down in Your healing waters. Help me find ways to allow You to fill the spaces they took with Your light and Your truth.

Master of the world fill me with humility and strength to do Your will. Take away my shortcomings – help me be free of the bondage of enslavement to them and allow me to continue on the journey towards standing at Mount Sinai, ready to receive Your Torah.

Please do not leave any defects behind – burn them away so that I may be fully cleansed of them. And when in the future whatever is left of them inside me begins to rise, may I know how to access Your wisdom to serve as the antidote. May I not let them have hold over me any longer.

May I turn only to You instead.

Source of Life, I am grateful for the gift of Your healing presence. I now place my life in Your care. See me. Feel me. Touch me. Heal me. Remove that which no longer serves me and fill me with Your presence, so that I may forever do Your will.

Amen.

Take in this moment, my friend. You have come so far on the road to recovery. I hope you can **feel new ways of being emerging in your life, and a sense of peace which you can access any time you need.** Remember this moment. Look around you, and breathe it in. Imagine God saying to you "yes, I accept your prayer, I forgive you, I love you, and I will be with you, now and forever" and anything else you can imagine God saying. Feel that deeply. Hold a snapshot of this moment in your mind that you can come back to in the future whenever you feel challenged or alone. Is there a quote or a song you can attach to this moment so you can remember it? I invite you to stay in this moment, take it in. This is a big step on your journey, and a good

111

preparation for the next part of the journey, which involves cleaning up your relationships with others you have harmed. I won't tell you that that's an easy part of the process. I will tell you that you've come so far, and with God's help, you'll probably be surprised at how much you can do. Let's see this process through, so that even more blessings can come your way.

Let The Teshuvah Begin!

Step 8: Made a list of all persons we had harmed, and became willing to make amends to them all.

Step 9: Made direct amends to such people wherever possible, except when to do so would injure them or others.

"A completely righteous man who never sinned is called holy, but a baal **teshuvah** who sinned and returned is called holy of holies, as Chazal said: "A completely righteous person cannot stand...in the place where baalei **teshuvah** stand."[56]

Teshuva and Yom Kippur only atone for transgressions between man and God...transgressions between man and his fellow, such as hurting his fellow, or cursing his fellow, or stealing from him, etc., those are never forgiven until he gives his fellow what he owes him, and [his fellow] is appeased. Even if he returned the money, he owed his [fellow], he must appease him and ask him to forgive him.[57]

Repentance is one of the greatest gifts of our lives. The ability to correct the errors of our ways places us even higher on the ladder of holiness than those who've never sinned. Why? Because they've never been tested, never had to look their ego and pride in the mirror and do the right thing even when they don't want to. It's hard to repent, it's hard to apologize. You have to be willing to look stupid and admit your wrongs. Having someone accept your amends is a blessing that makes it all worthwhile.

When I got to this step, I listed everyone I felt I had harmed in any way from my addictive tendencies. There were over forty names on my list. I reached out to each one I could find. My mother was deceased, so making an amends to her directly wasn't possible. Some people had no recollection of what I was calling them about. Some people told me I was a real jerk to them, yet they appreciated my reaching out, and a few of them I've reconnected with. I found every conversation valuable. Each one felt like cleaning up a layer of grease on the outside of my soul.

You will probably resist making amends, do them anyway. You might not want to work hard to find people, do it anyway, you'll thank me later, and you'll feel better too.

When I was in high school, there was a bookstore across the street from the school. I remember stealing pornography from the bookstore (I certainly wasn't going to buy it; someone might see me!). The bookstore is no longer in business. How could I make amends? After a few false attempts, I found the management company that owns the mall. I spoke to someone and asked if there was any information on the owners of the bookstore. They told me that the gentleman who owned the bookstore now owned the mall. I called his office and asked his assistant for ten minutes of his time. Needless to say, she was surprised that I had tracked him down to ask about the bookstore. I explained why I wanted to talk to him and asked her to set up a call. She eventually got back to me, saying that he felt that my efforts to reach out to him were enough, and that I was officially forgiven. I had been prepared to mail him a check or make a donation in his honor somewhere. I wasn't going to argue – if he was willing to move on, so was I (note to self: take yes for an answer!).

I have to share another story. Visiting a longtime family friend as a young adult, I ventured into their basement and came across a risqué novel, which was all about sex and illicit relationships. I stole the book and never told them. When it came time to make amends, they were on the list. They came to visit me, and over dinner I shared with them that I had stolen their book and felt bad about it. The husband looked up with a grin and asked why I hadn't taken the blow-up doll that was next to the bookshelf! While that was clearly not the reaction I had anticipated, we had a good conversation, they laughed about the whole thing and I felt better for owning up to my unfortunate behavior. I also gave them a gift card for them to buy a new book or two at their local bookstore. They said it wasn't necessary, and I insisted that it was necessary for me for them to have it.

I did include my family and my sponsor on the list (if only I had taken his advice sooner!). Shortly after making the list I found myself at a rabbinic conference, in a session on healing intergenerational trauma. We were all partnered up and invited to role-play a conversation with a loved one of ours. It immediately came to me that since I knew the partner was someone I could share with and skilled at spirituality and working with trauma, this was an opportunity to make an amends to my mother. We had the conversation – I said what I needed to, and my partner spoke to me as mom, accepting my apology, and offering her own for all the ways she hadn't been as supportive as she might have liked. It was incredibly moving, and very healing.

I didn't know that that conversation was going to happen. Interestingly, some of the people on my list came back into my life shortly after I made the list. It was almost as if the universe itself was supporting me on my mission. Maybe that was God's way of saying "attaboy, keep going".

Some amends took me longer to make. Some I dreaded, like the conversations with my first fiancée and my ex-wife. They each listened, said what they wanted, and I felt better for making the efforts to acknowledge that my addictive ways had impacted each of them negatively. It's not just that I could've been a better, more caring, more

116

loving partner, but I actually hurt them, and they didn't deserve to be the objects of my anger. I reached out to them both and asked if we might find time to connect. I was grateful for the opportunity to offer my apologies for my role in creating our dynamic. I felt better after having done so. I hope they did as well.

It is very easy, and very wrong, to make an amends while secretly having an agenda that they will also recognize the error of their ways and offer you their own apology (or your job back, your car keys, etc.). **An amends is only about repairing the harm that you have done to someone else.** If you have any other agenda it should be left out of the amends conversation. You don't want to have to make an amends for having poorly tried to make an amends. If you can't see that your actions contributed to the situation, you're not ready to make an amends. You also need not make amends for things that weren't under your control. Beware false grandiosity. You can only make amends for things you did which negatively impacted others. You will feel better when you do so.

Before you make the amends, ask yourself what it is that you need to make the amends for. What did you take from them? How did you harm them? Did you wound their pride, their sense of self? Did you steal their money or their dignity? Did you betray their trust? **Put yourself in their shoes and imagine how they must have felt when**

you harmed them. Remember that even if they are willing to meet with you, they're probably wondering why you've asked to meet them, and probably thinking you're going to say something hurtful to them. Be very careful about how you say what you say. If you are anything less than sincere, they will probably know it. Don't make an amends before you're ready. Talk with your sponsor, your coach, or your spiritual director and role-play the situation with them. Imagine how the conversation will go and practice saying the things you want to say. Write them down to take with you for the conversation – it's easy to forget and you want to make sure you say everything you need.

The person you are trying to make the amends to may not be ready to forgive you. They may need time to think about all you've said. That's okay. **Your job is to do the best you can to make amends, and they are allowed and entitled to respond however they feel is best.** Remember that you've time to think about making amends. They may need time to process and you will be well served by giving them whatever space they need. They may say that they can't forgive you. In that case, thank them for their time – arguing with them will do no good. Keep living a better life, and if it feels appropriate, revisit the issue in a month or in six months. Maybe they'll have had time to think about it and can find it in themselves to forgive you. That said, if they make clear the answer is no, and you ask them in a respectful manner on a few different occasions for forgiveness, it's probably time to let it go. You could ask for others help in convincing them to forgive you, and at some point, you will have done all you can do, in which case, just wish them well and ask God to bless them.

> "If his fellow does not wish to forgive him, he should bring a line of three people who are friends with him and they will approach him and ask [forgiveness] from him. If he does not give in to them, he must bring people a second and third time. If he still does not give in, they should leave him alone, and that person who did not forgive – he is the sinner. But if it was his teacher, he must come and go even a thousand times until he forgives him."[58]

Of course, **if you're going to make an amends you also need to show them that you are living life differently than you were before.** If you try to apologize for past behavior and then are still committing that kind of behavior, why should they forgive you? The whole point of the 12-step program is to become a better person. **"If I'm not better today than I was yesterday, then what do I need tomorrow for?"**[59] Is your teshuvah genuine?

> "What is *teshuvah*? It is when a person abandons the sin that he sinned and removes it from his thoughts and commits in his heart that he will not do it again, as it says, *The wicked should abandon his path* etc. (**Isaiah 55:7**). And also that he regrets sinning, as it says, *After I returned I regretted* (**Jeremiah 31:18**). And the One Who Knows Hidden Things testifies about him that he will never return to this sin, as it says, *And we will no longer call the work of our hands "god"* etc. (**Hosea 14:4**). And he must confess verbally and say these things that he has committed in his heart."[60]

If you stop making the work of your hands the thing you serve, if you open your heart and your life to allow God to direct you, then God will assist you in making teshuvah a part of your life. Can it happen that you do teshuvah and then make the same mistake again later? Of course. Hopefully if you've already done teshuvah you'll be much quicker to catch yourself and do teshuvah again. This program does not expect perfection – we all do the best we can, and there is nothing wrong with making an extra amends if we don't feel complete from the first one.

It is never too late to do teshuvah, not even on your dying day.

> "What is complete teshuvah?...when a person has the opportunity to commit the same sin, and he possesses the ability to do it, but he separates and does not do it because of teshuvah and not out of fear or lack of strength...And if a person only does teshuvah in the days of old age, when it is not possible to do what he once did...it is effective and that person is a ba'al teshuvah...Even if a person sinned all his days and did teshuvah on the day of his death and died in his teshuvah, all his sins are forgiven, as it says, Before the sun is darkened, and the light of the moon...This implies that if he remembers his Creator and does teshuvah before he dies, he is forgiven."[61]

Hopefully you still have years left to enjoy a better life. Even if you don't, we all want to end our days with a clean conscience and doing teshuvah before you die allows you to do so. That said, don't wait until you're almost dead to do teshuvah. "A person should do teshuvah from his sins immediately and not say...'When I grow old,

I will do teshuvah," lest he die before he grows old.'"[62] **Every day is a good day to make amends and begin a better life.**

If you stole money or property from someone, you must repay it. If you don't have the money, ask if you can pay them in installments or on a monthly payment plan. Your words of contrition are important and at the same time, if you owe them money, your words aren't enough. The same is true if by your words you caused them to lose money. "One who causes his fellow to lose money on account of slander, his repentance does not avail until he makes amends with him, whether by paying him or by beseeching him with words and humbling himself before them."[63]

There may be people for whom you can't make an amends, whether because they are deceased or because it would be dangerous for your recovery or harmful to them if you were to be in touch. If they are deceased, you might find someone to role-play, as I did, though it takes special training to be able to do that. I recommend you visit the grave of your loved one, or wherever their ashes are, and read a letter to them, and have the conversation you wish you could have had with them in person. While I have no way of knowing, I do believe they will hear you. Ask God for prayers on their behalf and give money to the favorite tzedakah or charitable organization of the one you are remembering.

If there are people who you would harm by making an amends, find another way to do so. For example, if you had an affair with someone, you harmed them and their family members. If their spouse doesn't know they've been cheated on, it would absolutely be inappropriate for you to offer to make an amends for an affair they don't know exists. That would just be causing them more pain. Write them a letter and read it to your sponsor. Ask God for prayers on their behalf and give money to the favorite tzedakah or charitable organization of the one you have harmed.

If there are people you can't be in contact with because it would harm your recovery, you might also write and read a letter to your sponsor, coach, therapist, or clergy. Maybe one of them or a recovery friend can be with you as you make a phone call. Maybe they can help navigate a way for the two of you to be in the same room safely. Obviously, every situation is unique, and you should never put yourself at risk of relapse and your safety is paramount. Still, if there are amends to be made, don't use this as an excuse not to make them. Use your support team and find a way, so that you can have the inner peace you deserve.

There may be people who wish to make amends to you. I encourage you to accept them. If you want others to accept your amends, it would behoove you to accept others as well.

"It is forbidden for a person to be cruel and not make amends; instead, a person should get appeased easily and get angry slowly. And at the moment when the sinner asks for forgiveness – forgive with a whole heart and a desirous soul. And even if he pained him and sinned against him many times, he should not take revenge or hold a grudge -- that is the way of the Children of Israel and their correct hearts."[64]

I know it may seem as if there are so many amends to make. Give yourself enough time for each one – don't try to rush the conversations just to get them off your list. **Authenticity and sincerity are key. Remember to treat everyone as they would want you to, and remember that they, like you, are a child of God, flawed and wonderful, all at the same time.**

As you go through your amends, you will likely remember more amends to make. That's natural - just add them to your list and keep going. I've met people who have literally made hundreds of amends, and they've all said that it's been worth it for them. No matter how many are on your list, be grateful for the opportunity you have to clean up your past and heal the relationships.

Most importantly, you must make sure that your efforts to do teshuvah are sincere and complete. Don't hold anything back (unless it would harm others), including your commitment to living a healthier way in the future. "Anyone who is prideful and does not disclose, but rather hides his sins – his teshuvah is not complete, as it says, one who covers his transgressions shall not prosper."[65]

Are you fully committed to walking away from the sins of your past?

> "Anyone who confesses verbally and does not commit in his heart to abandon [sin], this is like a person who immerses in a *mikvah* while holding an unclean creature in his hand, so that the bath is not effective until he sends away the unclean creature, and so it says, *One who admits and abandons is given mercy* (Proverbs 28:13). And he must specify the sin, as it says, *This nation has sinned a great sin and made a golden god for themselves* (Exodus 32:31)."[66]

"The essence of teshuvah is abandoning sin with a full heart and regret."[67] That said, there are different ways to do teshuvah, and you can work with your sponsor, coach, clergy, therapist, and/or recovery friends to find the best ways to make your amends and find strength and insight not to make the same mistakes going forward.

As you contemplate making amends, **don't forget to ask God for assistance.** Let God (and others) support you. You don't – and shouldn't – do this alone. "Among the ways of teshuvah are for the penitent to constantly shout before God with crying and pleading; and to do tzedakah according to his ability; and to distance himself very far from the thing."[68] Ask God for help discerning exactly how to make amends in each situation.

And then **make amends to God as well.**

How many times have you been angry with God for things that weren't God's fault? How often have you blamed God for the consequences of your own behaviors? How often have you shut God out of your life, and refused to allow God to be present? How often have you not thanked God for the blessings you have received?

It is so easy to be angry with God. We've all done it, and one could easily argue that in the face of today's realities, it's justified to be mad at God. And yet, it doesn't serve you to carry anger towards God. Find a quiet space, whether again in the mikvah, or in front of the ark in a synagogue, or on a mountaintop or hillside or forest, and talk to God. Apologize to God and invite God to come in again. I know you may think you've already done this earlier, and you have, yet doing so on a regular basis will remind you and God of your improving partnership.

After you've made amends to your friends, to your family, to everyone you've harmed, and to God, there is one amends left for you to make, and that, my friends, is to yourself. If you treated anyone else as poorly as you treated yourself, they'd probably ask you not to be friends anymore. You've been angry with yourself; you've not taken care of your body, you've put yourself down over and over, and you haven't been a friend to your own self. Now is the time to **take the compassion you are showing others and extend it into your own heart.**

I invite you to write yourself a letter, and then find a quiet space where you feel comfortable and safe and look at yourself in the mirror and read these words you've written. Tell yourself how proud you are of all you've accomplished. Apologize for all the mistakes you've made. Promise to do everything you can to support your own growth and development going forward. Place your hand over your heart, take a few deep breaths, look yourself in the eyes and repeat I love you for five minutes. Say it until your heart melts with compassion for yourself and then keep saying it. Make it a regular practice, as often as you need, even every day or several times a day is appropriate. Allow yourself to **fill yourself with love**. Show yourself the love that God has for you. Light yourself up with appreciation for your own beauty and uniqueness.

> "When a person does teshuvah out of love, the light of...the world...immediately shines upon that person."[69]

This, my friends, is the goal of recovery, and of life itself. **When you return to your best self from a place of love, you join with the great love of the world and light shines upon you.** You are filled with love and strength to keep going, to get through whatever challenges you face and to support others in their healing. **Love is the secret energy of the world, and it is the best energy, pure, vibrant, and holy.**

We addict have spent far too long living with fear, anger, sadness, jealousy, and despair. Now is the time to let the love shine into our lives, and to shine it back out into the hearts and minds of all we can reach. **When we love ourselves, when we love God, when we love the people in our lives, life itself gets better.** Let us commit to loving life, even with its challenges.

I once heard Rabbi Dovid Zeller, of blessed memory, speak. He asked what people loved and he noticed how many people said they love ice cream. There's nothing wrong with loving ice cream (unless, like me you're allergic to dairy and sugar and need to avoid it). He said, however, that even more than he loves ice cream, he loves the act of loving itself.

Isn't loving just the best?

It took me a long time to learn how to love myself. Some days, I forget and then I have to remind myself that I'm special and important, even with my flaws (I thank God every day that I'm blessed with my wife Sherri and with so many others who remind me that I am worthy of love!). I love to learn and to grow, and I love to learn about and with others. I love my wife. I love God. I love our cat. I love my siblings and family. I do my best to love everyone I encounter.

The poet Rumi said, **"Your task is not to seek for love, but merely to seek and find all the barriers within yourself that you have built against it."**[70]

Let us find all the ways we have distanced ourselves from love, and let us commit to loving ourselves, each other, God, and life itself going forward. Let the love revolution begin! I know it's not always easy, but it's definitely worth it. You won't love everything about every day. I don't. That's okay. We love as much as we can, each and every day. Life is a constant adventure in learning how to live from a place of love. I honor you for joining me in the journey. As my friend Shelley Goldberg teaches: You are love.

You are love.

You are LOVE.

YOU ARE LOVE!

Living Anew and Carrying The Message Forward

Congratulations, you've made it through the first nine steps. This is a fantastic accomplishment, and I hope you celebrate (in a healthy and sober way!) just how far you've come. Many people start the steps, not everyone finishes. The first nine steps helped you clean up your life and get connected with God and yourself. The last three steps help integrate all you've learned and set you on a great path for the life you want for the future. Even though these are the everyday maintenance steps, I encourage you to do some writing on each of them and bring that to your sponsor or coach. We never finish working the steps, yet when your sponsor or coach tells you you've successfully worked through all twelve steps, that is a moment worthy of celebrating. As always, the question is – how do you understand the steps, what do they mean to you, and how can you use them and fulfill them in a way that speaks to you and supports your life mission going forward. Everyone will do them differently. How can you use these steps to live well? Let's see how the last three steps can help live a life of recovery every day.

Step 10: Continued to take personal inventory and when we were wrong promptly admitted it.

In too much of the world today we think of apologizing as weakness. We're supposed to be the dominant ones, and anytime we admit we are wrong we're showing weakness. I think the opposite is true. **When we apologize for the errors of our ways, we're actually showing that we respect the person we're apologizing to, and that we are aware enough and humble enough to know that we make mistakes.** That is a sign of strength, not weakness. I am quick to apologize for errors I make, though I no longer apologize for errors I didn't make – why should I accept blame for something I didn't do? That said, when people express frustration to me, I will often say I'm sorry, or I'm sorry that happened. Saying I'm sorry (and meaning it) helps others feel heard and reminds me that I am here to help others (sometimes I get lost in my head. Asking how I can help others sets me free). If I think I've said something that might hurt someone, I will be quick to reach out, and even if what I said wasn't hurtful, it still gives me an opportunity to show the other that I care about them.

Don't hesitate to do teshuvah.

The opposite is also true. Just as we can be quick to offer an apology, being quick to accept someone else's apology is valuable. When we get angry, we often lose perspective. T. Harv Eker, founder of Peak Potentials Training, says "when emotions go up, intelligence goes down!"[71] In the Talmud they note that anger robs us of our scholarship. "Reish Lakish said: Any person who becomes angry, if he is a Torah scholar, his wisdom departs from him, and if he is a prophet, his prophecy departs from him."[72]

I am neither a scholar nor a prophet, yet I know enough to know that when I get angry, it can sideline me for days if not weeks. The longer I stay angry, the easier it is for me to head down the rabbit hole of emotions and addictive tendencies. I recommend that you set aside time each day, and each week to review your life. What has happened that went well? What can you celebrate? Who did you upset and how can you make it better? Who do you need to forgive? Rabbi Isaac Luria developed a bedtime forgiveness ritual. I find it extremely valuable to read these words, in whatever language you understand.

Here is a translation of his prayer by Rabbi Zalman Schacter-Shalomi.[73]

Ribono Shel Olam, I hereby forgive whoever has hurt me,

and whoever has done me any wrong;

whether it was deliberately or by accident,

whether it was done by word or by deed,

in this incarnation or in previous ones.

May no one be punished on my account.

May it be Your will, O Lord my God, and God of my parents,

that I sin no more, that I do not revert to my old ways,

that I do not anger You any more by my actions.

May I not do that which is evil in Your sight.

Wipe away the sins that I have committed, with Your great compassion,

but not through sickness or suffering.

May these words of my mouth, and the prayers that are in my heart,

be acceptable before You, O Lord, my Rock and my Redeemer.

Reb Zalman used to teach that **holding on to anger is like swallowing poison and expecting the other person to die.** When you forgive, you let go of the negative emotions inside you, and allow more space for your own healing. Try out this practice for a month, and see what changes come to pass.

You might also take time before Shabbat to let go of anything you don't want to bring into Shabbat with you. "Every Erev Shabbos you should examine your deeds, arouse yourself to repent and make amends for all the misdeeds you did in the six weekdays"[74]. I always want to go into Shabbat with a clean conscience. Taking the time on Friday afternoon to make amends, accept others apologies, and clean up any lingering emotional schmutz allows me to celebrate Shabbat with peace.

I encourage you, however, not just to promptly admit when you're wrong, but also to **promptly celebrate the good moments in your life** too. We are often quick to minimize the good things we do – it's important to make amends when we're wrong, and it's also important to build a healthy self-image, and we are allowed, and even encouraged to notice when things go well! I write down five good things that happen to me each day. I also share highlights with my wife Sherri, with my coach and sponsor, and at my meetings. If we only focus on the negative, we'll think that life is only about cleaning up the messes we make. If we learn to love ourselves more, we'll have less messes to clean up and life will be more enjoyable. That's worth celebrating in my book!

Step 11: Sought through prayer and meditation to improve our conscious contact with God as we understood God, praying only for knowledge of God's will for us and the power to carry that out.

Jewish tradition is full of beautiful prayers. Traditionally, Jews are invited to pray three times a day, but also throughout the day – when waking up, just before going to sleep, before and after meals, when seeing a beautiful view of nature, when reuniting with a long-lost friend, and whenever you can. The rabbis of the Talmud said we should pray for an hour before we pray, and then we should pray for an hour after we pray as well. Prayer (and Torah) should be our constant companions throughout the day.

The challenge is that many people don't speak Hebrew, don't like some or all of the prayers, don't believe in God, don't think prayer is important, and/or find the repetitiveness boring. It's easy to walk into Jewish spaces and think that prayer is all about reciting the same words our people have said for thousands of years, and knowing when to stand, sit, bow, and eat. I will be the first to admit that I find many prayer services hard to sit through. Where is the music, the story, the drama, the passion, and the yearning for a better world? Where is the inspiring call to lift ourselves and our world higher?

I agree with Rabbi Abraham Joshua Heschel who said:

"Religion declined not because it was refuted, but because it became irrelevant, dull, oppressive, insipid. When faith is completely replaced by creed, worship by discipline, love by habit; when the crisis of today is ignored because of the splendor of the past; when faith becomes an heirloom rather than a living fountain; when religion speaks only in the name of authority rather than with the voice of compassion - its message becomes meaningless."[75]

How can we make prayer more meaningful? A few suggestions:

First, **learn what the prayers mean, who wrote them, and why we say them**. There is tremendous beauty in the prayers and learning about the history and structure of the prayer service can help us have a more meaningful experience.

Second, **get involved with a prayer community**. I'm not saying you need to go three times a day, though I'm happy if you find meaning in doing so. My point is that we can all benefit from making prayer a regular part of our lives. It's often hard to find inspiration to pray on our own. **Being part of a community that shares an approach to prayer you resonate with can be very empowering.** If you're not sure what approach you might like, I encourage you to shul-shop, and visit a few different communities, ask people who pray there what they like about it and why it might be a good fit for you. It often takes time to see what you like about a synagogue, minyan, or havurah. In the recovery world, we tell newcomers to meetings to visit six times to see if it's a good fit. The same may be true of prayer communities. Try out a few and see if you can find the best fit for you.

Third, **don't just pray the words of the prayer book, pray the words of your heart as well.** The prayer book is a record of other people's yearnings to connect to God. We can benefit from praying their prayers, yet we need to add on our own. I've heard it said that **there are really only three kinds of prayers: Please. Wow. And Thanks.** What would you like to ask God for? What can you appreciate? What blessing can you offer? What hope for the world can you share? **Add your voice to the traditional prayers.**

Fourth, **when you're praying, ask for more than material things**. Heschel said "Never once in my life did I ask God for success or wisdom or power or fame. I asked for wonder, and he gave it to me."[76] Ask God to guide your steps, to bless the work of your hands, to be your partner in creating your life. Pray that God comes into your heart even more, and for wisdom, strength, understanding, love, and hope. All of that is worth so much more than just asking God for material needs.

Fifth, **don't pray that your problems will go away. Pray that you become bigger than your problems.** Your problems won't go away just because you want them to. Your problems will go away when your perspective shifts and you realize you have the skills to address it, and perhaps it's not even a problem, but an opportunity for growth.

136

Sixth, sing! "The primary purpose of prayer is not to make requests. The primary purpose is to praise, to sing, to chant. Because the essence of prayer is a song, and man cannot live without a song."[77]

"I Will Sing Your Strength
Extol Each Morning Your Lovingkindness
For You Have Been My Haven
And My Refuge in Time of Trouble
To You, O My Strength, I Will Sing."[78]

Seventh, **forget about whether God hears your prayers or whether your prayers will be answered. It actually doesn't matter. It's good for us to pray.** If God chooses to act on our prayers, that's great. When we pray from our deepest depths, energy shifts inside us. We open ourselves to the possibilities waiting to unfold. "Prayer may not save us. But prayer may make us worthy of being saved."[79]

Eighth, **don't let anything go unappreciated**. "Mankind will not perish for want of information; but only for want of appreciation. The beginning of our happiness lies in the understanding that **life without wonder is not worth living**. What we lack is not a will to believe but a will to wonder."[80]

Ninth, **pray YOUR way**. Chant, drum, sing, meditate, stretch, do yoga, walk in the woods, study Torah, read poetry, listen to music, be silent, laugh, make your whole life into a prayer. I once heard a lovely quote attributed to St Francis of Assisi: **"It is good to preach the gospel at all times. When necessary, use words."[81]** Make prayer your own, and mix it up whenever you feel your prayer life is growing stale. That's a normal part of prayer life. Don't be shy about changing things up to keep your prayer life fresh.

Tenth, **focus on the needs of the people in your prayer community. How can you serve them?** How can you help them feel more connected? Sometimes it's not the words of the page but the actions we do that make a difference. Don't ever take the people in your community for granted. Show up for them. Become the answer to the prayers they didn't even know they were offering.

"וַאֲנִי תְפִלָּתִי לְךָ ה' עֵת רָצוֹן
אֱלֹהִים בְּרָב חַסְדֶּךָ עֲנֵנִי בֶּאֱמֶת יִשְׁעֶךָ."

"As for me, may my prayer come to You, O Lord,
at a favorable moment;
O God, in Your abundant faithfulness,
answer me with Your sure deliverance."[82]

God wants your heart and soul. Your prayers are holy prayers. Your tears are holy tears. Your laughter is holy laughter. You are a prayer, your life is a blessing, and you are love. **Let God be a partner in your life and be open to the possibilities ahead.** You may be surprised at what can happen!

Step 12: Having had a spiritual awakening as the result of these steps, we tried to carry this message to alcoholics, and to practice these principles in all areas of our lives.

"אִם לָמַדְתָּ תּוֹרָה הַרְבֵּה, אַל תַּחֲזִיק טוֹבָה לְעַצְמְךָ, כִּי לְכָךְ נוֹצָרְתָּ."

"If you have learned a lot of Torah, do not credit it favorably for yourself, because for this you were created".[83]

The best way to ensure your own sobriety is to help others find theirs. You've benefited from others who have helped show you the way to a life of recovery. Now it's your turn to pay it forward and to help others in need. One of my colleagues says that you don't really become a rabbi until one of your students becomes a rabbi. I might adapt that and say you don't really become recovered until one of your sponsees becomes a sponsor. What I mean by that is **giving back to the program (whether you are a sponsor and also if you're not) and to others is a necessary part of the program and your recovery isn't complete without it.**

You can give back in many different ways. You can sponsor others and help them through the program. You can help organize or run the meeting. You can volunteer at the conference of your fellowship or with the world service office. You can edit the newsletter, help with finances, and more. Find what works best for you.

Most importantly, you can **be a light of healing to those who still suffer**. These programs are here to shift the consciousness and the energy of the world. In a time of such darkness, we need all hands-on deck to be spreaders of light. In this step you take your rightful place as a teacher and a guide for those people who you have the opportunity to reach. You don't have to write a book or teach about recovery in a wider setting – not everyone is called for that (though if you want to, I'm happy to help you do so). I know, however, that **there are people who only you can reach. There are people waiting for you to own the power you have to help them find experience, strength, and hope, one day at a time.** As you give to others, you'll likely find that the rewards come back to you a thousand-fold.

It's daunting to think about becoming a sponsor. What do I know, how can I teach others? The answer is you know enough to share the steps you took to get where you are now. Morgan Harper Nichols says "Tell the story of the mountain you climbed. Your words could become a page in someone else's survival guide."[84] You don't have to know all the answers. You have to be willing to serve, everything else will take care of itself. You can always ask your sponsor and other recovery friends for advice. **Ask God for help and help will be given, in the right way, and in the right time. Help others find recovery, and you'll find yourself as well.** When in doubt, give your sponsees the gift of unconditional love and support (not romantically, but in other ways). Everyone needs more love in their lives. Show your sponsees and those around you the love they wish they had received. Let love open doors for them and move them to a better place. "To love human beings is still the only thing worth living for; without that love, you really do not live."[85] "When in doubt, love more."[86] Good advice for your sponsee, your friends and family, and especially yourself.

As you serve others, this new person looking back at you from the mirror may surprise you. Welcome them with open arms! They've been waiting to come out for so long. Now is the time to celebrate them, to welcome your new self-home.

These twelve steps give us a daily reprieve from our addiction. So long as you keep working a program, you'll do fine. Thank you for giving yourself the freedom of recovery. You've invested time, money, and energy to get here, and I know we are all better off when any one of us takes steps to heal. Keep up the good work!

> "Our book is meant to be suggestive only. We realize we know only a little. God will constantly disclose more to you and to us. Ask God in your morning meditation what you can do each day for the one who is still sick. The answers will come, if your own house is in order. But obviously you cannot transmit something you haven't got. See to it that your relationship with God is right, and great events will come to pass for you and countless others. This is the Great Fact for us.
>
> Abandon yourself to God as you understand God. Admit your faults to God and to your fellows. Clear away the wreckage of your past. Give freely of what you find and join us. We shall be with you in the Fellowship of the Spirit, and you will surely meet some of us as you trudge the Road of Happy Destiny.
>
> May God bless you and keep you – until then."[87]

Love Your New Self
Every Day!

Wherever you are on your recovery path, I know you want to stay committed to it, each and every day. **As you work your program, you are literally building new pathways in your brain, replacing old patterns and beliefs with more supportive lessons to live by.** You are learning, just like I am, how to **give yourself the love that you may not have received earlier**, and how to **live life as a partnership between you and your Higher Power.** At a New Peaks conference, I attended, trainer Adam Markel invited us to "Let life support you."[88] We have been fighting life for so long, now we are embracing the joy of living.

In order to do that, we have to stay in dialogue with ourselves, and **love ourselves each and every day**. For far too long we have put ourselves down, belittled ourselves, and listened to the naysayers (ourselves included). Now we know that we must be kind, gentle, and loving with ourselves every day. We can set new goals, we can dream dreams, we can have bigger and better visions of ourselves, and we can accept ourselves just as we are. Author and speaker Mark Victor Hansen suggest we say to ourselves every morning and throughout the day "**I'm enough**."[89] I've certainly found that a much more empowering way to get through the day than belittling myself for all the ways I'm not perfect. A quote I love says **"when you argue for your limitations, you get to keep them. But if you argue for your possibilities, you get to create them."**[90] What empowering vision do you have for your future? What possibilities might await you?

It's often easier to love others than to love ourselves. Nevertheless,

> "it is mandatory upon every man to love each and every one of Israel even as he loves his own self, for it is said: 'But thou shalt love thy neighbor as thyself (Lev. 19:19).' One is therefore, obliged to speak in praise of his neighbor, and to be considerate of his money, even as he is considerate of his own money, or desires to preserve his own honor."[91]

In order to love our neighbors as ourselves, we have to start by loving ourselves. Is there a point at which we don't need to love ourselves? Can we ever cause so much damage that we're no longer worthy of love? Mussar teacher Isaiah HaLevi Horowitz, in his book Shnei Luchot Habrit, writes the following:

> "You may well ask how you can be expected to love your fellow Jew as yourself, when the reason you are to admonish him is that he commits transgressions which are apt to make you share in his punishment? The answer may be that we find many times that a person breaks his own hand or damages his own eyesight. He did not do so willingly, but the fact that it happened was a punishment for him. One does not stop loving

oneself because one has caused the loss of a hand or the loss of an eye. Similarly, one must not stop loving a fellow Jew who may have been or may become instrumental in causing one damage".[92]

I will take this teaching one step further. Even when we injure ourselves and there is no punishment at stake, we do not stop loving ourselves. **Until the day we die, we are to love ourselves and treat ourselves with the utmost care and respect**. We are children of God. As the popular saying goes, God doesn't make mistakes! Les Brown says we should think of the odds. 400 million sperm and we're the one that made it here![93] Clearly, God wants us to be here. Rebbe Nachman of Breslov said it too **"the day we were born was the day God decided the world couldn't go on without us any longer."**[94] **We are a masterpiece of heavenly creation, created in the likeness and image of God, and we are born to move mountains, to partner with God in healing the world, and to use all of our gifts in service of holiness.** "You shall be holy,"[95] we are told over and over again in the Torah. We must therefore treat ourselves in a holy and dignified way. We've only got one body in this lifetime. How we treat it affects our wellbeing each and every day.

When I was a child, I didn't like my body very much. I have flat feet, which made it hard to walk before I finally got orthotics. I have sleep apnea and was always exhausted for many years until I started using a CPAP machine. I had severe allergies and my nose was always dripping. I have asthma and a history of atrial fibrillation, an irregular heart rhythm, which caused me to overheat, sweat frequently, get dizzy if I stood up too fast, and prevented me from engaging in strenuous exercise. When I was a child, I wet the bed a lot and was teased for that as well as having a lazy eye and being overweight. It's no wonder I thought of my body as being defective – nothing worked right!

Thankfully, I've had surgeries to correct the atrial fibrillation, I use orthotics and a CPAP, I no longer wet the bed, I've cured much of my allergies, and I eat a lot healthier, avoiding flour, sugar, dairy, caffeine and alcohol (among other things), and I'm in decent shape. I still have a lazy eye, which confuses people, and allows me to see further to the left than most people. This comes in handy when I'm teaching school kids – they think I have eyes in the back of my head!

I don't tell you any of this to impress you. It's taken me a long time to learn that how I treat my body affects my wellbeing (and I have areas to improve still). **If I can make changes in my life, so can you**. Exercise is important, as it helps us eliminate toxins from our body and also releases endorphins, which helps with our mood. Given that so many of us sit for too many hours each day, even brief stretching every hour helps strengthen our core and prevents further damage to our head, neck, back, and shoulders caused by sitting too long. "Anyone who sits tight and does not exercise…even if he eats good foods and he guards himself according to [the dictates of] medicine - all of his days will be [full of] ailments and he will become weak."[96]

There are innumerable ways to exercise, from strength training in the gym to running, cycling, skiing, sports, yoga, kickboxing, walking, and so much more. If exercising intimidates you, start small and build up. I needed to hire a trainer to force myself to go to the gym. Otherwise, I just didn't have the motivation. I love going for long bike rides when I can get lost (and found) in nature. I love walking in the forest with Sherri or a friend. The change of scenery always does me good. Children (especially, though adults as well) today are spending less and less time outdoors, such that nature deficit disorder is a real problem. We spend our time tethered to our screens instead of connecting with others in the outdoors. I am no saint in this department – technology addiction is real and I have work to do on it. I know that anytime I'm out in nature, I feel free, which is never the case when I'm staring at a screen.

Whatever form of exercise you like, do it. "If your custom is to take walks, you should intend it for the sake of heaven – in order to be healthy for the service of God, blessed be He. Your thought should be that you are exercising so that your mind will be relaxed and vigorous, so that you will see how to act in all your affairs as is proper [that is, psychological health]."[97]

When I was twenty, I had the privilege of cycling from Seattle to Washington, D.C. This country is incredibly beautiful, and I realized on that ride that the human body is amazing. Here I was – an overweight, out-of-shape, nerdy Jewish kid who didn't know anything about cycling or the outdoors, cycling an average of seventy miles a day for ten weeks. If I can get in shape, so can you. Someday, I hope to hike the Appalachian Trail. I also want to run a marathon and climb Pikes Peak in Colorado Springs. I can't tell you how or when these will happen. I can only tell you that I intend to get as much mileage out of this body as I can. In order to do that, I have to watch what I eat, get enough sleep, and exercise. You might be wondering what this has to do with recovery from addiction. When our bodies are worn down, it is all too easy to reach for an addictive substance to help ourselves feel better. The HALT acronym mentioned in many recovery meetings and literature is helpful for us. It's wise not to get too hungry, angry, lonely, or tired.

How do you treat your body? Do you fill it with more food than it needs? Do you put toxic substances inside it? What are your exercise goals and what's your plan to achieve them? What steps can you take to have better health and to get closer to your goals?

147

Unfortunately, it's hard to be clear on what to eat. There are advertisements on seemingly every food telling you that it's the latest, healthiest fad. Even in health food stores there are foods with very high levels of sugars, starches, and saturated fat. I am not a nutritionist, or a doctor so please consult them before making any lifestyle changes. I can only say that getting off flour, sugar, and dairy was good for me. Drinking green smoothies each day has been good for me. Drastically increasing my vegetable intake has helped and increasing the amount of water I drink has as well. Most of us are dehydrated each day. Drink more water and you'll be surprised how much better you may feel.

We also don't sleep enough. We need seven to eight hours each day and it's a struggle for many people to get that much, myself included. There are so many things to do and so many distractions (television, Facebook, and more) and there is never enough time to spend with Sherri and other loved ones. On those rare days when I've slept more than seven hours, my energy is better and I'm more productive. Creating a healthy bedtime routine has been very helpful for me.

Exercise. Better nutrition and hydration. Sleep. These are all important. I also want you to prioritize art, music, poetry, culture, travel, and fun. **Life is too short for it to be boring and monotonous.**

Life is meant to be enjoyed. "Life is not measured by the number of breaths we take but by the moments that take our breaths away".[98]

Rabbi Abraham Joshua Heschel called this radical amazement.

> "Our goal should be to live life in radical amazement....get up in the morning and look at the world in a way that takes nothing for granted. Everything is phenomenal; everything is incredible; never treat life casually. To be spiritual is to be amazed."[99]

When was the last time you were amazed by something? When was the last time you had a moment that surprised you, that took your breath away? How can you bring more radical amazement into your life?

Heschel also said: "mankind will not perish for want of information; but only for want of appreciation. The beginning of our happiness lies in the understanding that life without wonder is not worth living. What we lack is not a will to believe but a will to wonder."[100]

When was the last time you asked God to surprise you with a wonderful experience? Admittedly, I don't usually either, though I like the idea and am starting to incorporate it into my life. I invite you to try it and see how it works for you.

For me, every time I make progress on a project I am filled with awe. When I lead communities in song and prayer, I am amazed at the sound of voices singing together. When I write or speak words that others find meaningful, I feel blessed. They're listening to me? (I've just written a book; how did that happen and how amazing is that?). When I coach people and watch them learning and growing into their best selves, I am overjoyed. Albert Einstein said, "there are only two ways to live your life, as though nothing is a miracle or as though everything is".[101] When I think about my own recovery journey, I feel truly astonished. Even a year ago, I couldn't have written any of this. Now, I am proud of how far I've come, and I can't wait to see where I go from here.

Take some time to think about your recovery story. Do you remember what you felt at your lowest point (whether that was a day, a week, or years ago)? Can you think of a few moments where you've felt blessed, where you've been astonished by the magnitude of life? Write those moments down, remember how they felt, call them up in your minds, and savor the experience. When you feel disconnected, return to those feelings. Schedule some time for a new adventure. Surely (I hope) you can find at least an hour a week to go for a walk or a drive in a new direction. Use those vacation days, and if that's not possible, go online and watch movies about places you hope to visit someday. **Let life inspire you, each and every day.** It's easy to fall back on our addictions when we're bored and uninspired. Make a habit of experiencing life as a great adventure and you won't be as tempted to fall back into old patterns.

Jewish tradition invites us to say one hundred blessings every day. There are blessings for getting dressed, before and after eating, for seeing oceans and rainbows, and so much more. I invite you to come up with blessings in your life. When I'm stuck in traffic and late for a meeting, I say a blessing when the traffic starts moving. When I see a beautiful sunrise or sunset, I say a quick blessing. It doesn't matter if you don't speak Hebrew – you can offer God blessings in any language. I often say them in English. Sherri and I say blessings before every meal, and after them as well. I always express gratitude not just for the food, but also for whatever feels alive in me at the moment. Our tradition has so many blessings and they've too often become rote. We need to reclaim our own power to **make new blessings, and to offer the gifts of our hearts and souls to God.**

What are you grateful for in this moment? Offer a short prayer to God. Here are a few suggestions but feel free to create your own.

Dear God, I'm so grateful for.....

Dear God, thank you for........

Hi God, I don't even know if you exist or if you're listening, but thanks for what just happened today....

Higher Power, thanks for guiding me on my recovery....

Source of Life, thank You for bringing the right people into my

life to help me grow.

Pray from whatever place your heart is in. If you're mad,

sad, or angry, you can pray from that place too. I guarantee you God

can take it. Sometimes we need to get it all out. Go for it!

My favorite blessing is Asher Yatzar, the blessing we say after

using the bathroom.

"בָּרוּךְ אַתָּה ה' אֱלֹקֵינוּ מֶלֶךְ הָעוֹלָם אֲשֶׁר יָצַר אֶת הָאָדָם בְּחָכְמָה וּבָרָא בוֹ נְקָבִים נְקָבִים
חֲלוּלִים חֲלוּלִים. גָּלוּי וְיָדוּעַ לִפְנֵי כִסֵּא כְבוֹדֶךָ שֶׁאִם יִפָּתֵחַ אֶחָד מֵהֶם אוֹ יִסָּתֵם אֶחָד מֵהֶם
אִי אֶפְשַׁר לְהִתְקַיֵּם וְלַעֲמוֹד לְפָנֶיךָ. בָּרוּךְ אַתָּה ה' רוֹפֵא כָל בָּשָׂר
וּמַפְלִיא לַעֲשׂוֹת."

"Blessed are You, Lord our God, King of the universe, Who
fashioned man with wisdom, and created within him many
openings and many cavities. It is obvious and known before
Your throne of glory, that if but one of them were to be
ruptured, or but one of them were to be blocked, it would be
impossible to survive and to stand before You. Blessed are
You, God, Who heals all flesh and acts wondrously."[102]

Here's an interpretive translation by Rabbi Zalman Schachter-

Shalomi:

"I worship you, Yah, our God, Cosmic Majesty, You formed
me, a human being, so wisely. You created in me all kinds of
hollows and ducts, inner organs and intestines. As I am all
transparent to You, it is apparent and clear, that if any of these
that need to be open would clog, or any of these which need to
be enclosed would seep, I could not exist and live in Your
sight, not even for a moment. So I am grateful and bless You,
for healing me, in amazing ways."[103]

We've all been sick, some of us more than others. What a blessing it is that our bodies work at all! When was the last time you were grateful for the things you currently take for granted? Can you put more radical amazement into your daily routine and find time to appreciate things more than you currently do?

A story is told of Hillel that when he finished a lesson with his pupils, he accompanied them from the classroom. They said, "Master, where are you going?" He answered, "To perform a mitzvah." "Which mitzvah is that?" they asked. "To bathe in a bathhouse," replied Hillel. The students asked, "Is this a mitzvah?" Hillel replied, "If somebody is appointed to scrape and clean the statues of the king that are set up in the theaters and circuses and is paid to do the work, and furthermore, associates with the nobility, how much the more so should I, who am created in the divine image and likeness, take care of my body."[104]

Each day is a new opportunity to love your self, to be grateful, and to praise God for creating you, and the world and all it contains. How awesome and wonder-ful it is just to be alive. For me, spending time in nature is the easiest way to have a sense of wonder, though I am also amazed at the love and connection I find in relationships with the people (and animals) I love.

Rabbi Nachman of Bratzlav used to spend time each day in the outdoors. This was one of his prayers:

153

Master of the Universe,
Grant me the ability to be alone;
May it be my custom to go outdoors each day
Among the trees and the grass, among all growing things,
And there may I be alone and enter into prayer,
To talk with the One that I belong to.

May I express there everything in my heart
And may all the growing things of the field
Awake at my coming,
To send the power of their life into the words of my prayer,
So that my prayer and speech are made whole,
Through the life and spirit of growing things
Which are made as one by their transcendent Source.

May they all be gathered into my prayer
And thus may I be worthy to open my heart fully
In prayer, supplication, and holy speech,
That I pour out the word of my heart before Your presence like water,
And lift up my hands to You in praise,
On behalf of my own soul and the souls of my children[105]

May we also merit the opportunity to open our hearts fully, to elevate our souls in gratitude and prayer, to express the yearnings of our hearts , minds, bodies, and souls, and may we be made whole in the process of returning to our deepest essence, the Oneness of God. As we return to our Source, may we be healed, and inspired to keep shining and radiating light and warmth back into the world. May we inspire others, and may we know peace.

Lay Your Losses Gently Down

"There is nothing so whole as a broken heart"
– Rabbi Menachem Mendel of Kotsk[106]

Here's an unfortunate truth we all need to accept at one point or another: **everyone gets sick, and everyone dies**. I know that this might seem obvious to us, yet so often when we experience sadness of any kind, we habitually numb ourselves out with our addictions. Even people who aren't addicts will often turn to food or alcohol or shopping as a coping mechanism when hearing bad news. Unfortunately, as a society we haven't learned how to talk about death, sadness, illness, and suffering in healthy ways, and there's probably nothing that will trigger a relapse like death or illness of a loved one or of oneself.

The news is full of depressing reading. Good people are dying every day from war, disease, famine, gun violence, wildfires, car accidents, environmental disasters, and more. How can we possibly remain calm in a world so full of tragedy and sadness? What right do we have to even be happy when so many others are sad? Why doesn't God prevent such terrible things from happening? Why don't we?

How we choose to respond to the challenging realities of our life determines more than we think. Do we reach for a bottle at the sign of bad news or do we reach for the phone to call our sponsor or a friend? A friend of mine just said the following: "drinking is not the answer, but when you drink, you forget the question."[107] Of course, when the alcohol wears off, the question is still there waiting to be answered.

Theologians have struggled to explain why bad things happen to us for as long as humans have been alive. I don't believe that God causes car accidents or cancer or other disease, and I also don't believe that death is a punishment for our sins. Death just is, and short of cryogenically freezing ourselves, there seems to be nothing we can do about it except accept that someday everyone we love, and we too, will die.

The best thing we can do in times of sadness is to allow ourselves to fully feel our feelings. Too often we think we need to be strong for others, and that if we cry, we'll never stop. There are times when parents need to be strong in order to keep taking care of their children, and at the same time, everyone needs an outlet to let go of our sadness and tears. If you let them out in a healthy way, you will find healing and a lessening of your sorrows.

My father, Rabbi Mel Glazer, of blessed memory, was both a congregational rabbi and a grief recovery specialist. He wrote:

> "There are (only) 3 steps from grief to healing:
> 1. Accept the loss
> 2. Cope with the loss
> 3. Embrace the new life you have created. Nothing will be the same, but it won't hurt so much, and you will be able to look back and remember your loved one, and move forward to a life filled with joy and celebration."[108]

I see so many people, myself sometimes included, arguing with reality. If I don't allow myself to grieve, if I don't acknowledge they died, then on some level they're still alive. At least I have my pain, which is a reminder that they existed. It's natural to want to find ways to carry our loved ones with us. Sometimes, however, that desire keeps us stuck to them in unhealthy ways. **We are meant to mourn, to grieve, and to wrestle with the sadness and the absence of those we loved**. When we don't deal with those challenges, we carry those emotions inside us, festering away, waiting to be heard. Years ago, I was spending Shabbat at a permaculture village in Costa Rica. I saw a man in his early 20's who had a most intricate necklace. It looked like an ornate pouch around his neck, with bright blue and purple colors. I told him I thought it was beautiful and asked if there was symbolism to it. With tears in his eyes, he told me that it contained his mother's ashes. My heart immediately went out to him. Clearly the pain of his mother's death was still with him. He wanted to be close to her, and I honor him for that. At the same time, I suspect he was preventing

himself from doing the hard, emotional work of laying his mother

gently down, mourning her in his own way, and going on with his life.

My father used to say that **the secret of mourning is that we**

didn't die, by which he meant that when death comes, those of us who

remain are still alive, and still entitled to happiness, health, and a life

worth living. Obviously, we need to mourn our losses and Jewish

tradition gives us many wonderful tools to do so. Still, just because our

loved one is sick or has died, we must not give up on the hope of a

better tomorrow. We can hold on to their memories, even as we still go

forward.

Rabbi Abraham Joshua Heschel, one of dad's teachers at the

Jewish Theological Seminary, taught that "there are three ascending

levels of mourning: with tears - that is the lowest. With silence - that is

higher. And with song – that is the highest."[109] I pray that God gives us

strength to mourn, to cry, and to sing a new song, a song that emerges

from the broken places of our hearts and lifts us up to new heights, and

a song which holds the memories of our loved ones close to us,

allowing us to call upon them whenever we need.

Of course, not all sadness comes from death. The promotion

that never came, the romance that fizzled out, the children moving

away, hunger, homelessness, poverty, abuse, and so much more. Can we be happy even amidst the disappointments? It's not always easy, and yes, we can still find a way to be happy. **"The only thing that keeps us from happiness is searching for it."**[110] What if we stop looking for happiness and just allow ourselves to be happy right now?

Happiness is a choice. Always putting ourselves down, comparing ourselves to others, and staying in misery is also a choice. Unfortunately, we think we're supposed to be miserable all the time, yet when do we allow ourselves to be happy? President Abraham Lincoln said, "most people are about as happy as they make their minds up to be".[111]

What does happiness mean to you? Do you allow yourself to be happy? Under what circumstances? How do you express your happiness? When can you be sad? Who can you turn to for support when life feels overwhelming?

It's not always easy to find support when you're feeling down. It's easier to isolate, to drown our sorrows away, to live life from a place of perpetual misery. "Life's hard, that's just how it is." "I'll be happy when I get the promotion, when the kids move out, when I retire, when I get all my ducks lined up in a row." Tony Robbins teaches that when we tie our happiness to our expectations and our expectations don't take place, we train ourselves to be miserable. We can choose to find things to appreciate each day. We can train ourselves to let happiness come into our lives. We certainly do not have to be sad every

moment of every day.

Rebbe Nachman of Bratslav said:

"in general, one must try with all one's might to be joyful always. For it is human nature to be drawn to bitterness and sadness because of the wounds one has suffered-and every person is full of troubles. So, one must force oneself, with a great effort, to be happy always…Now, it is also true that a broken heart is very good-but only at certain times. So, it is wise to set an hour each day to break one's heart and talk to God, as we do. But the rest of the day, one must be in joy."[112]

The longer we go without experiencing joy, the harder it is to find it again. Perhaps the only way to get out of our suffering is to invite God to bring us more joy. Rabbi Kalonymous Kalman Shapiro, the Rabbi of Piasetzno and the Warsaw Ghetto wrote:

"There are times when the individual is astonished at himself. He thinks: Am I not broken? Am I not always on the verge of tears – and indeed I do weep from time to time! How then can I study Torah? How can I find the strength to think creatively in Torah and Hasidism? At times the person torments himself by thinking, 'can it be anything but inner callousness that I am able to pull myself together and study, despite my troubles and those of Israel, which are so numerous?' Then again, he will say to himself, 'Am I not broken? I have so much to make me cry; my whole life is gloomy and dark.' Such a person is perplexed about himself…God, blessed be He, is to be found in His inner chambers weeping, so that one who pushes in and comes close to Him by means of studying Torah, weeps together with God, and studies Torah with Him. Just this makes the difference; the weeping, the pain which a person undergoes by himself, alone, may have the effect of breaking him, of bringing him down, so that he is incapable of doing anything. But the weeping which the person does together with God – that strengthens him. He weeps – and is strengthened; he is broken – but finds courage to study and teach. It is hard to raise one's self up, time and again, from the tribulations, but when one is determined, stretching his mind to the Torah and Divine service, then he enters the Inner Chambers where the Blessed

Holy One is to be found; he weeps and wails together with Him, as it were, and even finds the strength to study Torah and serve Him."[113]

Our suffering is a pathway to God, if we push on it, asking it to reveal its secrets. We might even find that God is there weeping for us and with us, and that knowledge might soothe our tears and give us the strength to go on. "In the darkest hour the soul is replenished and given strength to continue and endure".[114]

If you find yourself in a dark time, don't despair. Search for meaning, and for those who can support you during this time. Go to a meeting and share. Talk to your rabbi, your minister, your imam, or your faith leader. Talk to your coach. Call a friend or a loved one. Don't act out – you've worked so hard to get to this place and now is not the time to let that all go. Allow yourself to feel your feelings. I know you have it within you to go forward, even with any sadness you carry. You may want to seek counseling. You may want to do bodywork to remove trauma from the body. There are many different healing modalities – find what works for you and allow yourself the gift of healing.

When I find myself in difficult times, I try to remember other difficult times I've been in, and then I remind myself that if I can get through that, I can get through this. I'm strong, I have the tools of the program, and I can ask for help from others. Whatever emotion I'm feeling is not worth ruining my sobriety. On the contrary, this too is an opportunity to strengthen my sobriety and to allow God even more into my life.

I bless us all that when the sorrows come, we find meaning and healing, and a way forward to the light of wholeness and a greater connection to ourselves, our loved ones, and God.

"The whole world is a very narrow bridge. The most important thing is to not to make ourselves afraid."[115] Let us turn to God in our hours of need and find comfort in God and in each other. The Adon Olam prayer invites us to place our trust in God:

"בְּיָדוֹ אַפְקִיד רוּחִי בְּעֵת אִישַׁן וְאָעִירָה
וְעִם רוּחִי גְוִיָתִי אֲדֹנָי לִי וְלֹא אִירָא."

"Into Your hands I entrust my spirit, When I sleep and when I wake;
And with my spirit, my body also; You are with me; I shall not fear."[116]

May we all be blessed with the strength to endure the challenges of life, and may we find in them healing, connection, love, joy, and peace.

Find Your Joy!

"עִבְדוּ אֶת ה' בְּשִׂמְחָה בֹּאוּ לְפָנָיו בִּרְנָנָה."
"Serve God in Joy – Come before God in song."[117]

What is the goal of recovery and all forms of personal

transformation?

The big book of Alcoholics Anonymous states

"we are sure God wants us to be happy, joyous, and free. We
cannot subscribe to the belief that this life is a vale of tears,
though it once was just that for many of us. But it is clear that
we made our own misery. God didn't do it. Avoid, then, the
deliberate manufacture of misery, but if trouble comes,
cheerfully capitalize it as an opportunity to demonstrate His
omnipotence."[118]

For many of us, the only joy we knew was that of our

addiction. Our home lives were broken and dysfunctional, our work a

daily trudge to survive. When we picked up that cigarette, that bottle,

that needle, that pill, that brownie, the remote, that romantic partner,

finally we found relief from all that ailed us, at least for a moment in

time. The only problem with these solutions is that the minute we stop

using them we are back to where we were, just as miserable as before,

if not even more so. Deep down we know these solutions can't heal what ails us, and we blame ourselves both for not being strong enough to stop using them, and for the damage we've done to others in order to maintain our habits. The guilt and shame compound upon each other, and we despair of ever finding real happiness and serenity.

It is no surprise, then, that giving up our addictions is an excruciating choice to make, even as it's necessary. **In order to find real happiness, we must stop holding on to the imagined happiness. We must give up our story of who we are now in order to become who we can yet be.** We must stop telling ourselves that we deserve one more episode of acting out because of how special we are. We must **stop listening to the voices that tell us we'll always be worthless addicts** (or whatever you tell yourself), and this is just who we are. When we surrender and find communities of support to help us navigate the program, and when we commit each day to showing up as our best selves; that, my friends, is worthy of a (healthy, and sober) celebration.

My coach tells me, and I tell the people I work with, that it's important to **celebrate all wins, no matter how little**. Every time I made an amends, I was grateful for the blessings I received from another moment of repairing my life and the damage I'd caused to another. I spent years avoiding medical debt, furious that the insurance companies had refused to pay for things that should've been covered. I owed thousands of dollars in unclaimed medical bills. I didn't even

want to open the envelopes – I couldn't face what lay inside. When I

finally committed to digging myself out of the mess I had made, every

time I paid off a bill, whether it was for $10 or $1,000, I celebrated. It

is good to know that I don't owe anyone money today. My credit score

improved tremendously when I paid off my debts. I celebrate that too.

It's easy to be hard on ourselves – we addicts are used to

dwelling in misery and sadness. It's much harder to reclaim joy and

gladness. One of the ways we do that is by accepting that we always

have a choice as to how we respond to situations.

> "Rabbi Eliyahu Dessler (d. 1953), one of the great Mussar
> teachers of the 20th century, sharpens this concept of free will
> in a way that accounts for nature and nurture. He writes that all
> humans have free will only at something called a
> Bechirah/Choice point. To explain this idea he offers an
> example of a smoker. The smoker coughs heavily at night and
> cannot sleep. He promises himself that he will not smoke again
> the next day. The next morning he thinks, "I'll have just one."
> He knows from experience that once he smokes that first
> cigarette he craves a second and cannot stop. However, he
> believes the thought, "I'll have just one," and lights up. Of
> course, he ends up smoking a pack and lies awake coughing
> that night only to repeat the whole exercise the next day. The
> Bechirah point was the moment he chose to listen to the voice
> that said, "I'll have just one." According to Rabbi Dessler, the
> truth is that he can never stop at one. He has a choice between
> truth and falsehood."[119]

When I used to go grocery shopping, it was inevitable that

something I knew was bad for me would end up in my shopping cart. I

would walk in and tell myself that I was only going to buy healthy food, no more of that garbage I kept eating. And inevitably, I'd come to the snack aisle or the freezer section, hesitate, debating what to do, and then I'd go down the aisle, telling myself, just this once and then I'll change my ways. Giving up peach sorbet was one of the hardest things I've ever had to do, and I'm glad I did. For a long while I had to choose not to go down those aisles, knowing that I'd be tempted if I did. Now if I'm grocery shopping and I see a snack I used to eat; I remember what my sponsor told me: "Nothing tastes as good as sobriety feels." I offer thanks to that snack for getting me through hard times and I congratulate myself for not needing to buy it anymore.

The lie I used to tell myself was that I needed those foods to be happy, and I deserved them for all the good I was doing in the world. Those thoughts were addictive, and they kept me stuck in my own misery. **It's impossible to be happy when you've decided that your happiness is dependent on something else.** Rabbi Simcha Zissel Ziv, another Mussar teacher, said that "A truly happy person does not allow his happiness to be dependent on any external factor over which he may not have control"[120].

In order to be happy, I needed to stop giving my power away to other people, places, and things. I then needed to fill myself up with new habits and hobbies that would bring more joy into my life. In my case, I started going to the gym three times a week. I celebrated every time I could exercise longer, faster, or smarter than I could the previous time. I went on long bike rides. I joined a Toastmasters club and went every week, working on improving my speaking skills and celebrating my accomplishments and those of my fellow club members. I listened to music, read books, ate well, got more sleep, travelled, and allowed myself to enjoy my life. Can I tell you that every day has been fabulous since? Of course not. I can say that making joy a regular part of my life has drastically improved my mood and helped me stay focused on my recovery. "A joyful heart makes for good health; Despondency dries up the bones."[121]

What did you enjoy as a child? What did you always want to be when you grew up? What new habit or skill have you been putting off? In what situations do you feel despondent? How can you think about them differently to let go of the stress and find more joy and serenity? How do you talk to yourself when things go differently than planned? Are you critical of yourself on a regular basis? When was the last time you looked yourself in the mirror and said I love you? (I dare you to try that for five uninterrupted minutes each day. Look at yourself in the eyes and say I love you every few seconds. Breathe it in. Release the self-doubt and criticism. Let love fill your heart and soul).

Are there days still when I am overly harsh on myself? Absolutely. In those moments, I call my wife, or a friend and they remind me I'm a good person (and/or give me encouragement, perspective, and when needed, a gentle metaphorical kick in the rear if I'm not being as good a person as I could). I try not to stay too long in those negative thoughts. There is nothing gained from me dwelling on how miserable I sometimes think I am. It's not true, and it just keeps me locked in sadness and victim mode instead of being empowered to make things happen in my life.

Rebbe Nachman of Bratzlav knew a lot about sadness and suffering. He said, "one must search out and seek to find in himself some modicum of good, in order to revive himself, and attain joy".[122]

What are five things you like and appreciate about yourself? I encourage you to make a list at the end of each day of five accomplishments or appreciations from that day. Train yourself to start looking for things to appreciate. Wayne Dyer said, "change the way you look at things, and the things you look at change."[123] **Start finding more joy in your life, and your recovery will improve.** "Sing to God", and yourself, "a new song"[124] of love and kindness and watch what happens.

When you start seeing this joy show up in your life, notice it, appreciate it, breathe it in. It may feel strange – what is this thing called happiness? Let it come and play with it. How can you use it to grow through your challenges? How can you bring even more of it in your

life? Where have you been holding back from letting joy in?

When you do find joy, don't just keep it to yourself - share it
back with God, and with those around you. Rabbi Levi Yitzhak of
Berditchev, a famous Hasidic rabbi, wrote that

> "joy in one's heart...is bound to subside and cease altogether in
> short order...by giving verbal expression to one's joy and
> composing a song and writing poetry one prolongs and
> intensifies this feeling of joy."[125]

You can also choose to share that joy with others who may not have

access to joy themselves. According to the Talmud, it may even give

you a place in the world to come!

> "Two brothers came to the marketplace. Elijah said to Rabbi
> Beroka: These two also have a share in the World-to-Come.
> Rabbi Beroka went over to the men and said to them: What is
> your occupation? They said to him: We are jesters, and we
> cheer up the depressed. Alternatively, when we see two people
> who have a quarrel between them, we strive to make peace."[126]

How can you use humor and joy to spread peace in the world?

According to several Jewish teachings, we are obligated to be

joyful. Rebbe Nachman said:

"מִצְוָה גְּדוֹלָה לִהְיוֹת בְּשִׂמְחָה תָּמִיד."

"It is a great Mitzvah (Commandment) to be Happy at All Times."[127]

Can we really be happy at all times? Of course not. Death, illness, and

tragedies happen regularly. Sam Crowley, host of the Every Day is

Saturday podcast, says "you're either just out of a crisis, going through

a crisis, or headed towards a crisis".[128] Our lives are bound to get uprooted and impacted by the news of the world (which itself is often

depressing). I am not a fan of artificial happiness and putting on a

happy face even when you're not (though of course there are times

when we need to). Nevertheless, I believe that **even in times of great**

sadness and sorrow, there are also moments of great beauty, and if

we are on the lookout for them, they can help ease our pain and allow

us to more quickly find joy again.

In the Torah God specifies what will happen to the Israelites if

they don't follow God's teachings. Interestingly, God says that if they

don't serve God in joy, they will be punished severely. "Because you

would not serve the Lord your God with joy and gladness over the

abundance of everything".[129] Maimonides takes this a step further:

> "The joy which a person derives from doing good deeds and
> from loving God, who has commanded us to practice them, is a
> supreme form of divine worship. Anyone who refrains from
> experiencing this joy deserves punishment, as it is written:
> 'Because you have not served the Lord your God with joy and
> a glad heart'".[130]

Let us resolve to find more joy and gratitude for all the

blessings in our lives. Even when things don't look in our favor, let us

still find ways to celebrate the ability to wake up each day, the friends

and loved ones who support us, and the beauty of being alive. You can

find joy in nature or from your pets, and you can find joy in the gift of

Torah study. Rabbi Moshe Chaim Luzzatto said this about joy:

"This is the true joy, namely, that a person's heart delight that he merits to serve before the blessed Master, of whom there is none like Him, and to toil in His Torah and His mitzvot...for the further a person merits to enter into the inner chambers of knowledge of His blessed greatness, the more his joy will increase and his heart will sing within him."[131]

If you find yourself in a place where your heart is not singing, ask yourself what's bothering you. Is there sadness or pain you are holding on to? Where does it come from and does it still apply to today's situation or is it just a habitual pattern? Can you breathe into that sadness, honor it, and let it go? Are you trying to control a situation that's not working out in your favor? Are you annoyed when other people aren't playing the parts you want them to play? Remember a recovery adage, which some call the 11th commandment: "Thou shalt not take thyself too damned seriously!" My wife is very good at knowing when I'm up in arms over something I can't control. She reminds me that I'm not the center of the world (thank heavens), and that the world won't end if something happens differently than I want it to. It may even turn out better than I thought! Regardless, my own peace of mind is worth more than holding onto an expectation. This doesn't mean that I can't go back to someone and ask for clarification or offer a different approach or share a disappointment, it just means that I'm willing to accept that there are other ways to make things happen than whatever I thought of. **Surrender your expectations, and joy can more easily follow.**

"Rabbi Yishmael says: Be yielding to an elder, pleasant to a youth, and greet every person with joy."[132] There are so many people in the world who don't experience joy on a regular basis. Can you share with them some of yours?

"Through joy, peace comes to the world."[133] When we find our joy, we are more peaceful. When we are more peaceful, we don't get as easily triggered, and we fill our lives with people and moments that take our breath away and fill us with gratitude for the gift of life itself.

"זֶה הַיּוֹם עָשָׂה ה' נָגִילָה וְנִשְׂמְחָה בוֹ."
"This is the day that God has made; let us be glad and rejoice in it!"[134]

May we all find the joy that is our heritage and our birthright. May we use that joy to help inspire ourselves, and others, to new heights, so that all can know joy, and so that all of us, and the entire world, can know joy and peace.

Celebrate Shabbat
And Holy Time

"More than the Jewish people have kept Shabbat;
Shabbat has kept the Jewish people."[135]

"Judaism teaches us to be attached to holiness in time, to be attached to sacred events, to learn how to consecrate sanctuaries that emerge from the magnificent stream of a year. The Sabbaths are our great cathedrals."[136]

This book would be incomplete without a brief mention of the wonderful day that is Shabbat. From sundown Friday night to the stars coming out on Saturday night (roughly twenty-five hours), Jewish tradition invites us to experience an oasis in time. On Shabbat we celebrate the joy of living. We eat with our family and friends. We are nourished by our communities in the synagogues and in our homes. We give ourselves a break from the world, to recharge and renew ourselves. The Torah says that God worked for six days to create the world, and God rested on the seventh day. So too, we are instructed to work six days and rest on the seventh.

Many people get bogged down in the many laws of what to do and what not to do on Shabbat. This chapter is not meant to be a guide for which rules to follow. Consult your rabbi, members of your spiritual community, or any of the many books, videos, and learning opportunities about Shabbat. What I am here to say is that **Shabbat is one of the greatest gifts you can give yourself.** It probably sounds counter-intuitive – if we're here to make the world better, then why should we take a day off from doing that work? The answer is to remind ourselves that **the job of saving the world is not ours alone** – others can do their share as well, and furthermore, we need to appropriately replenish ourselves in order to keep giving the best of ourselves to the world.

There are many different ways to keep Shabbat. A meal with family and friends, with candle lighting, challah and wine, blessing the children, and singing songs of Shabbat is certainly a wonderful option. Many people love going to services. Many people don't, and that's okay too. Some people love to spend time in nature, which they wouldn't be able to do during the week. Some people like to sleep late and go to shul for lunch. Some people go to shul and then take a long nap. I love to sing holy music on Shabbat, whether in synagogue, around the table, or on my own.

I do my best not to use technology on Shabbat. In today's interconnected world where we're always on the go, it is quite a gift to have twenty-five hours where I need not be attached to my cell phone and email. There is an unfortunate rise in the use of cell phones by some religious teens (and others) on Shabbat afternoon. They call it keeping half-Shabbes.[137] Mostly they just want to be connecting to their friends and I understand that (though I suspect that some are also addicted to their cell phones and find refraining from technology for 25 hours too much to bear). I just wish they – and we – would find time to connect in person. Communicating from a distance or online only goes so far. **Shabbat is a time to catch up with our loved ones, to inquire about their week, to just enjoy their presence and appreciate the blessing they bring to our lives. What a gift it is to have meaningful, holy conversations.**

I invite you also to **give tzedakah before Shabbat begins.** In my house growing up, any change we had left over from the week went into the tzedakah box. As a family we would decide every now and then where to send it. Giving tzedakah became ingrained in me and linking it to Shabbat reminded me that **as blessed as I am, there are people who don't have the blessings I do.** Give tzedakah before lighting the Shabbat candles, and then enjoy your Shabbat – let yourself be renewed – and then continue working after Shabbat to make sure that one day we will have a world where no one is poor, and all can celebrate with their loved ones.

The gift of Shabbat is the gift of rejuvenation. This is a gift we all deserve. I invite you to make Shabbat a regular practice, in whatever way makes sense to you and your family. If there is no community where you live, you can watch a service on a livestream. You can listen to music or go for a walk together with your loved ones. Reach out to your loved ones before Shabbat and give them a blessing and let them know you love them.

Of course, I encourage you to celebrate not just Shabbat, but all the Jewish holidays. Passover invites us to work towards greater freedom for us and for who live on earth. Sukkot reminds us to that the world is fragile and our blessings come from God. On Shavuot and Simchat Torah we honor the wellsprings of wisdom we receive from Torah. Hanukkah helps us find light in the darkness of our lives. Rosh Hashanah and Yom Kippur call us to do teshuvah, to begin again, to reorient our lives, recommitting ourselves to a life of holiness. These (and the remaining) holidays keep me grounded in Jewish time. When I celebrate them, I feel connected to Jewish tradition, to my family (including my parents and grandparents), to the Jewish people, and to God. The Jewish calendar is beautiful and holy and gives an added layer of meaning to my life, and many opportunities to increase the holiness I yearn for.

176

I invite you to make Jewish holidays your own. In my opinion, Shabbat is probably the best gift God gave to the Jewish people. Welcome others to your home and give yourself and others the gift of Shabbat as well. **The world needs us all to slow down and remember why we are here, not just to fix what's broken, but also to celebrate what works**. When we appreciate the gifts we have, more will come our way.

Being in recovery does add some challenges to the Jewish calendar. As I've mentioned before, wine on Shabbat and most holidays can feel challenging to those who don't drink. For those who've given up sugar, even grape juice can be a challenge. Jewish law is clear that there is never an obligation to eat or drink anything that is harmful to our health. I stopped eating challah years ago when I became gluten-free. While there are gluten-free challahs, they often have so much sugar added that it's not healthy for me to eat it. I'm okay with this, and at the same time, I can appreciate everyone else's enjoyment of food I don't eat myself. Still, celebrating the holidays is a gift in my life, and I hope they can be in yours as well. If you want to be holy, our tradition gives us many ways to do so, and celebrating holy time has to be at or towards the top of the list. Shabbat and holidays remind me that God is holy, that all of God's children are holy, and that I am holy too. And so, my friends, are you!

Who's on Your Recovery Team?

"לֹא טוֹב הֱיוֹת הָאָדָם לְבַדּוֹ."
"It is Not Good for Humankind to be Alone."[138]

When God created Adam in the Garden of Eden, God quickly decided to make for Adam someone who could accompany him on his journeys. God decided to make "a fitting helpmate"[139] for Adam. God created Eve, and together they had children, explored the Garden, connected with nature, and got into a whole heap of trouble by listening to the snake and eating the forbidden fruit of the tree they were told not to eat from. Still, according to Jewish tradition Adam was lonely in the Garden, and God realized that loneliness is not a good condition for spiritual growth, not for Adam, nor for us.

We can't recover, or live healthy lives, in isolation. We simply must have others in our lives helping us make sure we're on the right track. I talk to my sponsor weekly, and more often when I need him. He makes sure I'm working my recovery program and helps advise me when I have questions and/or when I'm not sure how to approach a situation. I have a coach I work with twice a month. She helps me gain clarity on my life goals and what I need to stay at the top of my game (and how to dust myself off when I'm not). I talk to my Spiritual Director for an hour every month. She makes sure my soul is in the right place. I talk to recovery friends almost daily. I go to meetings at least once a week. I stay in regular contact with my small circle of friends. I spend as much time with my wife as possible.

As I said before, sometimes it feels like it takes a whole village just to keep my head on straight, and that's true. I'm grateful to everyone on my "brain trust". Recovery is partly a disease of isolation. When we are alone, it is too easy to think we are worthless, incompetent schlemiels who aren't worth love and connection. When we give in to those thoughts, not only do we make it easier to reach for our comfort foods, bad habits, and addictive behaviors, we also rob ourselves of the connections we truly want with others. When I stay in my head too long, doubt, fear, sadness, low self-esteem and negative self-worth too often arise, accompanied by an ever-expanding to-do list, which only seeks to remind me how incompetent I feel, and the cycle continues.

It's not good for us to be alone. Recovery teaches us that **others share the same problems we do.** We're not as messed up as we think we are, and when we let others into our lives we **give ourselves**

opportunities for real human connection. It is good to know how to be alone with ourselves, and at the same time **we must have a solid support system to help us when days are tough, to celebrate with us when things go well, and to inspire us to keep climbing ever higher.**

Who's on your support team?

Who do you want to include in your life?

Who inspires you to keep growing?

Who can you reach out to when things get tough?

Who would reach out to you for support when they need a hand?

It is my hope that readers of this book will support each other's growth. Keep reading to find ways to do so. Let us always remember that we're never alone, and that together, we can achieve miracles, one day at a time.

Keep Learning Forward!

We all want to make progress in our recovery, and in life. The only way to do that is to keep learning. Motivational speaker Charlie "Tremendous" Jones said that:

"You will be the same person in five years as you are today

except for the people you meet and the books you read."[140]

When I wake up in the morning, I offer gratitude to God for the gift of another day, I look over at my wife and feel blessed to share my life with her, and then I open a daily recovery reader which has short inspirational thoughts for each day of the year. I want to begin my day in the right frame of mind – the news of the world can wait. Making sure that my soul is ready for this day is crucial. Recommitting to my recovery program, each and every day, helps ensure that I stay on the right path.

I always have a recovery book I'm reading. Sam Crowley, speaker and host of the Everyday is Saturday podcast, says that we all need to be reading thirty minutes a day. Learners are earners. You may not be able to read for thirty minutes, so start with five minutes.

Everyone can find five minutes to learn instead of watching television, scrolling Facebook, or numbing out with other distractions. Thankfully today you can listen to audio books if that's easier for you.

I listen to a lot of podcasts about recovery, spirituality, personal growth, and finding meaning in the world. Whenever I'm in the car, exercising, washing dishes, doing laundry or other chores, I fill my mind with as much wisdom as I can. There are certainly times I watch television and scroll Facebook. I've noticed, however, that I feel more empowered after listening to and learning from a podcast then I do from just watching television or listening to the radio. If you fill your life with only the depressing news of the world, you won't think the world can improve. If you listen to empowering content, you'll know that you have a part to play in making the world better for all.

Les Brown and his students host a Monday night motivational call that's free and full of wisdom. I host the Torah of Life podcast, where I bring you Jewish wisdom to help you live better, happier, healthier, and holier lives. Subscribe today at https://www.blubrry.com/torahoflife/, on iTunes, or on your favorite podcast player.

There are at least ten daily emails I get which bring me inspiration and recovery wisdom. Hazelden, Daily AA emails, Napoleon Hill, Bob Proctor, Neale Donald Walsch and others give you daily wisdom to inspire you. I'll be happy to share the list with you. It will be available at www.facebook.com/ourjewishrecovery and at www.andgodcreatedrecovery.com. Feel free to send along others you like and I will add them to the list.

Of course, I have colleagues I study Jewish texts with as well. Currently I study with two different colleagues, studying the weekly Torah reading and commentaries. I'm always looking for inspiration within Jewish tradition, and I share what I've learned on the Torah of Life podcast, and in my writings. I also especially like reading works of mussar. According to the Mussar Institute,

> "Mussar is a path of contemplative practices and exercises that have evolved over the past thousand years to help an individual soul to pinpoint and then to break through the barriers that surround and obstruct the flow of inner light in our lives. Mussar is a treasury of techniques and understandings that offers immensely valuable guidance for the journey of our lives.
>
> The Jewish community spawned Mussar to help people overcome the inner obstacles that hinder them from living up to the laws and commandments—the mitzvot—that form the code of life. That community tends to see Mussar as inseparable from its own beliefs and practices, but the human reality Mussar addresses is actually universal, and the gifts it offers can be used by all people[141]."

T. Harv Eker, founder of Peak Potentials Training (now Success Resources America) says that "whatever you focus on, expands".[142] If you fill your life with empowerment and recovery, you'll feel more empowered and your recovery will be stronger. **Every day we can choose to live an empowered, recovered life.** If we fail, let's just pick ourselves back up and keep going. Don't let yourself go days at a time without reading – your recovery will suffer, and you may go down a road you don't want to be on. **Keep reading, keep learning, and keep growing, each and every day.**

I love venturing into used book stores to see what treasures I might find. That said, I've learned that just buying the books doesn't make me smarter if I don't actually read them! Jim Rohn said "the book you don't read won't help"[143] and I couldn't agree more.

I love attending seminars and attend as many as I can. I like personal growth retreats, recovery conferences, Jewish learning and holiday gatherings, and any environment, which will allow me to expand my knowledge base and find like-minded people to learn from and with. These conferences have pushed me out of my comfort zone – I've walked on hot coals, swallowed fire, gone skydiving and more. These actions remind me that if I can do that, I can do whatever obstacle I'm facing. Of course, there are many conferences where they will try to sell you every program under the sun in the name of your learning. I've invested in many such courses, and they've all been valuable, some more so than others. As I get older, I am much more discerning about what I sign up for. I'm vastly more interested in the nuggets of wisdom, which will change my mindset than another program that promises riches in return for little work. As an entrepreneur, there are absolutely times when I invest in education and training to take my business to the next level, and I'm not shy about admitting that I need help to make my visions a reality.

Every recovery fellowship has an annual conference, and many have local events a few times a year as well. I can't recommend these highly enough. Unfortunately, there is not always an organized Jewish presence at these retreats and being Shabbat-observant (and keeping kosher) can often be a challenge. That said, it's usually worth the challenge. JACS hosts an annual retreat or two. I hope to help organize more of them in the near future. Sign up for my email list at www.andgodcreatedrecovery.com to be notified of when the next Serenity Shabbat will be taking place.

How much time can you invest in your own learning? Five minutes a day? Ten? Thirty? Do you prefer to learn with emails, podcasts, books, conferences or a combination? Who can you learn from to help move you forward with your life goals? **When in your day can you find 15-30 minutes to read or listen to inspiring and educational content?**

Look up the next annual conference and regional gatherings for your fellowship – when are they next meeting? Can you attend at least one conference per year?

Are you journaling or taking notes on what you learn along the way? What are the keys lessons you've learned over the course of your recovery? If you were to write a book about your experience – what three lessons would you pass on?

Who are you learning with? Ecclesiastes says:

"...טוֹבִים הַשְּׁנַיִם מִן-הָאֶחָד"

"two are better than one, in that they have greater benefit from their earning. For should they fall, one can raise the other; but woe to the one who is alone and falls with no companion to raise him![144]"

For many of us, myself included, it's hard to be disciplined on your own. Who in your network can you learn with? Who can you grow with? Find a recovery learning partner and commit to a regular check-in, even if it's once a week, to go over your learning together.

Can't find a group? Visit www.andgodcreatedrecovery.com and www.facebook.com/ourjewishrecovery to see what we're learning and when. Join us as we study wisdom to propel us forward.

Please note that you'll probably want to change your learning every few months. The same book you've been reading will grow stale. Take a break from it. Find something new to inspire you. There is so much wisdom out there to be found.

Whatever you do, don't stop learning. Make sure to share your learning with others as well. You may be surprised when something you say can open to a door of healing for another person.

Keep learning forward!

Watch Out, Challenges Ahead: Common Obstacles on the Recovery Journey

Everyone experiences challenges on the road to recovery. If you think that changing your life from the inside out is easy, you're in for more than a few surprises. In fact, even if you know that recovery is a lifelong path to healing, odds are good you'll still be surprised by the highs and lows, the oys, the joys, and everything in-between of recovery. This is why I fill my life with as much recovery and healing as possible. I need the added reminders to live as holy a life as possible.

Relapses are common. Old habits die hard. Even as I am amazed at how far I've come, I am still constantly amazed at how much work I still have to do just to be happy and healthy, grounded and centered in the world. I need to keep my recovery in mind whenever I contemplate a new job or commitment. Is it safe for me to attend that meeting? Can I maintain my sobriety if I attend that event? Will my recovery be threatened if I take that new job and if so, what can I do to give myself extra support? After four years of recovery, these questions are second-nature to me, and I've also built up enough strength that I don't respond to all the triggers I used to. I'm stronger than I've ever been, and I owe much of that to recovery. I don't want you to think that you'll need to be looking over your shoulder every minute for the rest of your life. At the beginning of my sobriety, I absolutely needed to call my sponsor often to help me navigate difficult situations. I still appreciate his wisdom when I'm unsure how to proceed (and we still talk at least once a week), for which I am immensely grateful.

A new colleague invites you to have a drink after work. An old acquaintance calls to tell you they'll be in town and wants you to celebrate his engagement at the local strip-club. Thanksgiving dinners, Passover Seders, and other holiday meals with way too much food for anyone to eat. Family vacations to the beach. These kinds of challenging situations will inevitably occur in your life. How we respond to the unexpected is what matters. Do you get easily frustrated and angry with others or do you respond with kindness and compassion even when things don't go your way? How do you handle the unexpected?

When the unexpected arrives, try to remember this wise guidance: "A person who has mastered peace of mind has gained everything".[145] It is so easy to lose our peace of mind, and so hard to get it back. **We all have situations that trigger us. We all experience challenges. We can let those challenges anger us, or we can let them remind us that because of our unique circumstances we need to spend more time making sure we have what we need. When in doubt, be proactive!** When I stopped eating gluten, sugar, and dairy, I had to relearn what to eat! We didn't have many vegetables in the house growing up. Now, they make up a substantial part of my diet. My friends and loved ones also needed help figuring out how to feed me. On many meals, I became upset and frustrated when there was little, I could eat. Now, instead of getting frustrated I make sure to be in touch with the hosts ahead of time and send them a list of everything I can and can't eat, with suggestions of what they might make for me, and offering to help cook. Gary Vaynerchuk says that "everything wrong with my business is my own f'ing fault".[146] The same is true with our recovery. **It is our job, for the rest of our lives, to keep ourselves on a solid recovery path. We can ask for help, yet at the end of the day it's not anyone else's responsibility to meet all of our needs** (especially if we haven't even told them what those needs are).

Here are some common obstacles people in recovery might face:

Challenge: My family and friends don't support me.

They say I'll never change.

It is quite common for addicts in recovery to have earned themselves a negative impression from their family. Addicts tend to steal, lie, cheat, and evade responsibility for their actions. They may cycle in and out of recovery. Is it any surprise their families might not think they can change their bad habits?

My advice: **Don't talk about your recovery to everyone right from the start, and don't expect anyone to think differently of you after you go to one or two meetings.** There are a lot of people who go to a few meetings and then we never see them again. Keep going and keep living and working your recovery to the absolute best of your abilities. When your family sees you acting differently, thinking differently, treating them with the kindness and respect you may not have shown them before, they'll probably come around. If they don't, you'll still be better off for cleaning up your life.

Challenge: My family and friends don't support me.

They say I'm changing.

You don't need anyone's blessing to improve your life with the gifts of recovery. If you stop drinking, your friends at the bar will probably no longer be your friends. That's okay, you'll make new ones. Your old friends may even be mad at you – they probably know deep down that they need to change as well, but they don't want to do the hard work to make it happen. When you change they are reminded that they need to change, and they don't want that reminder and instead of dealing with their frustrated desire to change, they can just be mad at you instead and drink until they forget that nagging feeling that they can be better. You will lose some friends, and that's okay. Author and humorist P.G. Wodehouse said, "the usual drawback of success is it annoys one's friends so."[147] You will make new friends who will support your growth and well-being.

If you need to, I suggest you walk away gracefully. Don't get mad. Don't try to reason with them. If your friends can't support you growing and healing, wish them well and go heal. You will absolutely find new friends as you recover. You will be sad when friends disappear – many marriages crumble when one partner goes into recovery. Many business partnerships dissolve. Careers are shifted. That's okay. Keep your head down, work your program, and stay focused on your recovery goals. The right people will support you along the way, and you'll be amazed at the blessings you'll receive along the way.

Challenge: I haven't hit rock bottom yet.

This is just my opinion, but I think this is one of the silliest things I hear in recovery rooms. It is an unfortunate belief that too many people have that you have to hit absolute rock bottom before you can get better. In my experience, **there is never a better time than**

right now to move in the right direction. In recovery rooms, some

people talk about having a high bottom, and some people have a low

bottom. Some drinkers get drunk after one beer and some people need

to have seven or eight before they get buzzed. Some sex addicts get

help after realizing that pornography has interfered with their life, while

some people frequent massage parlors, spend thousands of dollars on

prostitutes and video chat, get arrested for under age solicitation, and

spend time in jail. Some overeaters get help after gaining a lot of

weight. Some people get help quickly, and some spend years thinking

they can handle it, in and out of jails, hospitals, and rehabs before

finally surrendering to the program. Sadly, many never surrender and

die before getting help. "I haven't hit bottom yet" really means I'm not

ready to give up my addiction yet. Why not? How is your addiction

serving you? Do you not think yourself worthy of recovery? Are you so

used to giving up on yourself that you can't imagine a better way? Are

you convinced you'll die on the street, and it doesn't matter when or

where? Your life is valuable, and you can make it through. Help is

available. Now is a great time to turn your life around.

A story is told of a young boy walking through his

neighborhood, when he sees an elderly gentleman sitting on his porch,

a dog at his feet. The boy notices the dog lying on the porch, growling

in pain every few seconds. The boy asks the man why the dog is growling, to which the man responds that the dog is lying on a nail. Why doesn't he move, the boy asks. The man responds that the nail doesn't hurt him enough for him to move.[148]

How much pain do you need to be in before you say enough is enough? How bad does your life have to get for you to surrender your pride and ask for help? If not now, when? Get the help you need. You won't regret it.

Challenge: Other people have it worse off than I do.

Really? So what? **There will always be people worse off than you. There will always be people better off than you. Your recovery isn't based on anyone else. If you need help, get it.** I had a therapist in college who said, "just because you're drowning in the bathtub doesn't mean you have to care that it's not the ocean".[149] If you're drowning, you're drowning. As Marianne Williamson says: "we have suffered enough".[150] I'm glad you're aware that others have it worse. It's good to keep that in perspective. And the best thing you can do for others is to get yourself well. When you do, you can then focus on giving back to others however you wish. You deserve recovery just as much as anyone else.

Challenge: I don't have time to work a recovery program.

Interesting. Everyone has twenty-four hours in a day. The average American spends several of those watching television and scrolling Facebook. You can't find an hour a week to attend a meeting? You can't give yourself five or ten minutes a day to read recovery literature and start working a program? Of course, you can. **When you say you don't have time, what you really mean is this is just not a priority for you right now.** I don't mean to sound harsh, but **for this program to work for you, you have to commit to it.** There are miracles waiting to happen, some fast, and some slow. When you **devote as much time to staying sober as you did to maintain your addiction,** your life will be significantly improved.

I do know that people are busy, and the demands of work, children, and medical challenges can be incredibly taxing, which is all the more reason why you need to give yourself an hour a week to have an oasis of sanity amidst the storms of life. I listen to recovery podcasts as I drive to and from work. There are recovery meetings you can call into by phone on your lunch break (though I recommend in-person meetings when possible). If you make time for recovery, you'll find the time in your schedule to make it work for you, and you'll be better off for it.

Challenge: I don't want to work a recovery program any more.

How long do I need to do this? When do I get better?

You get better every day you work a recovery program.

How long you want to stay in recovery depends on how long you want to live well. Here's the thing – I don't want to go to meetings either. I don't want to call my sponsor. I want to be able to eat every food I can without gaining weight. I want enough money to not have to work the rest of my life. I keep going to meetings and calling my sponsor and working my program because I know that this way of living is infinitely better than the pain and desperation of my previous years. I know that I don't want to go back to life the way it was. I've come too far, and I'm not willing to give up on the dreams and goals I have for my self and my future. I've noticed that when I stop going to meetings, I also stop exercising, and then I make poorer food choices, and then I gain weight, and then I feel bad about myself, which can lead to poorer food choices, until I finally realize that I've gone down the rabbit hole again and need to clean up my act. When I start trying to give myself excuses, that's the time I need to recommit. The longer I go between meetings and conversations with my sponsor and recovery friends, the harder it is for me to get my head back in the right frame of mind.

I hear your desire to not want to have to do this anymore. For better and for worse, this way of living allows us to be the best versions of ourselves. Why would you want to stop doing that? Think about the pain you experienced before getting into recovery. Remember the alienation, the loneliness, the frustration, feel it deeply. Next time you pick up a cigarette, a drink, a cookie, or your drug of choice ask yourself if it's worth it. **Is it worth all the pain and aggravation to have one more?** I know for me the answer is clear. As we say at the end of meetings: Keep coming back. It works if you work it, so work it, you're worth it!

Challenge: I'm not getting better. It's not working for me.

How long have you been in the program, a few weeks? A month? Six months? Recovery takes time and effort. Are you doing everything you can to work a program? Do you have a sponsor and a coach you talk to frequently? Do you go to meetings and share what's going on in your life? Do you talk to other recovery friends regularly? Do you read recovery literature? If you're not doing these things you have no right to say it's not working, since you're not working the program. If you are doing these things, give it time. **Miracles don't usually happen overnight.** Have you stopped the offending behavior? That's progress. Are you thinking a little more clearly? That's fabulous. Are you kinder to yourself and to the people you work and live with? That's incredible.

I felt a lot better about my own recovery when I started seriously working the steps. It took me three years to get through them. You can do it faster, and I recommend that you do. I know I rebelled against the program, complaining and bemoaning that I still needed to do this work. When I stopped complaining and just did the work, I felt a lot better and made significant progress on my recovery.

If you really feel that it's not working for you, talk to your sponsor or coach. If you don't have a sponsor, find someone at a meeting who has significant recovery and who you resonate with and ask them to be your sponsor. Maybe you need more than one meeting a week. Maybe you need a therapist to assist. Maybe you need medication. Maybe you need to find a different meeting or even a different structure to your recovery program. And maybe you need help seeing the progress that you're already making. Are you still sober? Excellent, you're making progress. **Wherever you are on your recovery journey, don't stop until the miracle happens. It will.**

You might also **ask yourself what progress looks like for you.** What has to happen for you to decide you're making progress? Do you have to have worked the steps before you feel you've made progress? Do you have to be the most recovered in your meeting? Is that true, or is that just what you've told yourself? And how did you even decide that in the first place? Accept who and where you are, keep working the program, and it will work for you. If it doesn't, reach out to me directly and we can find time for a free consultation.

Challenge: Other people are doing better than I am.

Excellent. Ask them what they're doing and follow their advice. **You can learn from everyone who is working a program.** However, **if you're always comparing yourself to others, you are probably always going to find yourself wanting.** (You may also be wrong in your comparisons. You're only hearing what they tell you. Are you really hearing all of their struggles?) Everyone uses the tools of recovery in their own way. No one is better than anyone else. Your job is to give yourself as much love and compassion as you can while asking others for help and supporting others as best, you're able. Often, we see other's successes and vacation photos on Facebook, and we compare our failures to their successes and wonder why we're so miserable. Maybe we should all post our failures on Facebook too! That's probably unwise, yet we need to be comfortable with who we are. If others are doing worse than us, we can help them. If they're doing better, we can emulate them. Either way, we can keep learning and growing.

Challenge: I want to create my own recovery program that works for me. The ones out there aren't my style.

What is it about the current program that isn't working for you? Many people don't stay in programs because they're hard work. Some people leave because they don't want to follow the rules. Some people leave because they can't stand listening to other people talk and just want the whole room to listen to them for an hour. Do any of these describe your situation? If so, then the problem isn't the meeting, it's your inability to follow directions.

That said, 12-step recovery is not the only way to get recovery. You can absolutely create a recovery program that works for you, and your sponsor (which you should have regardless of which fellowship you're in) can help you figure out what's right for you. Unless your particular addiction hasn't been discovered by anyone else yet, I would strongly advise you against trying to create your own programs. It's hard to do and if you're just getting into recovery, you're in no position to instruct others how to work a recovery program. I couldn't have written this book until after working the steps and spending years on my recovery. Get clean, get sober, join a fellowship, a coaching program, or another healing program (or all three) and get healthy. If after doing so you still think your particular needs aren't being addressed, share your ideas with others in recovery, get feedback, and go ahead and create them.

Challenge: I don't believe I'll ever make it.

Maybe I am just a worthless screw-up after all?

That sad story you've been telling yourself for way too long keeps you stuck in old patterns. If you've read this far I know you have it in you to get healthy. Remember all of the reasons why you want to do this – your loved ones, your friends, your desire to be free, and your vision for who you can be in the world. Focus on who you are becoming and remember that others have made it through and so can you. As Les Brown says "you've got something special. You've got greatness in you.[151]" Put another way, God doesn't make mistakes. If you're here on this planet it means you're supposed to be here. **I know you have what it takes to get through this.** If you'd like extra support, reach out to me directly and I'll do what I can to help. In the meantime, start with one thing every day that contributes to your recovery. Make your bed. Do the dishes. Call a recovery friend. Exercise. Walk in the woods. Don't stop until the miracle happens. It will if you keep hanging on long enough. If I can do it, you can do it too!

It's important to know that even when you work a recovery program, old patterns and beliefs will come up. When that happens, you might say "thank you for sharing. Next!" A friend of mine says "that's my addict talking again." Just because thoughts come to you doesn't mean you have to act upon them. Every day you can choose which thoughts to let go of and which to embrace. Choose wisely!

Challenge: I can't believe all the crazy and stupid things I've done.

I'm so ashamed of myself. Why should anyone forgive me?

It's great that you know you have some things to address. Many people don't even know that so congrats for being self-aware enough to know that you've hurt some people and you'll need to make amends to them. The truth is, some people may never forgive you. Most people absolutely will, if they see that you're making a concerted effort to turn your life around, and if they see that you're genuinely sorry about what you did to them. Your sponsor will help you know when you're ready to start making amends (that happens in step nine – do the steps in the order they're in and you'll get there). Please don't make amends before your sponsor tells you you're ready. You may inadvertently make the situation worse. Reread the chapter on step eight and nine before making amends. Just know now that **most people want to forgive you and you can and will get better if you keep working the program.**

Challenge: I can't believe I relapsed again.

Why am I so bad at this?

Welcome to the club, my friends. These things happen. Pick yourself back up, call your sponsor, go back to a meeting, and begin your recovery again. It took Thomas Edison over three thousand tries to create the light bulb. When he was working on creating a battery, after over nine thousand attempts, his friend Walter S. Mallory visited him and asked: "Isn't it a shame that with the tremendous amount of work you have done you haven't been able to get any results?" Mallory writes: Edison turned on me like a flash, and with a smile replied: "Results! Why, man, I have gotten lots of results! I know several thousand things that won't work!"[152]

The question is not whether you will have a perfect recovery from the moment you start. The question is how will you treat yourself when the (hopefully rare) slips happen. Progress, not perfection is the rule of thumb. Instead of beating yourself up and asking what was I thinking, ask yourself what was I learning instead. Why did you just slip? What happened to cause you to act out? The better you get at identifying your patterns, the easier it may be to change them. **No one has perfect recovery. We're all a work in progress until our dying days.** Treat yourself as you'd treat another friend in the recovery rooms – with compassion, kindness, and encouragement to keep going.

Challenge: I'm addicted to multiple things. Where do I start?

Those of us who are cross-addicted have extra layers of recovery to work through, and it's totally worth it to do so. My answer to your question is to **start with the recovery program that will give you the most benefit**. Is there one addiction that you turn to the most? Is there one that is most threatening to your wellbeing? Start there.

I feel your pain on this question, as I myself am cross-addicted. In my case it was clear to me that love addiction and pornography was the area I needed to focus on. I've also spent time working on my codependency tendencies. While my eating has improved, I still intend to focus the next round of my recovery on that, followed by technology addiction and skin-picking. At some point, you just have to choose somewhere to start, though I encourage you to see if there are small ways you can improve on your secondary addictions even while you're working on your primary one.

I will add, however, that at least for me, as I worked through my primary addiction, my mind became clearer and I started treating myself with more kindness and compassion. This will be invaluable as you work on the other addictions as well. Brian Tracy teaches that we should "Eat that frog," by which he means we should tackle the most difficult task first, and then the remaining ones will be easier since we'll already have accomplished a bigger task.[153] Others teach that you should start with the easiest thing in order to have a small win and build up from there. Personally, I like Brian's advice, though I agree that building and celebrating small wins is a necessary part of the program. If you were to call me (or anyone else) on the phone and tell me what your biggest recovery challenge is, what would it be? When you know that answer, you'll know where to begin.

Challenge: I get triggered when I'm with family, at work, around my kids, on the holidays, and in other situation. What do I do?

We all have triggers. Recognizing them ahead of time and making a plan for how to keep your recovery and your sanity is key. Many people get especially triggered by family celebrations, which may contain alcohol, sugar, foods we need to avoid, and family members who aren't supportive of our recovery. It may be that you need to stop going to family gatherings for a while until your recovery is strong enough. Your sponsor, coach and recovery friends can help you set a plan on how to address other family members and make sure your needs are met. If you don't think there will be food you can eat, discuss ahead of time with your loved ones and bring your own if necessary. If you know that your family likes to eat and then all gather for drinks, maybe join them for the food and leave before the drinking starts or bring your own non-alcoholic beverages. Is there another member of the family you can ask for additional support ahead of time? Who's your favorite family member who you trust? Can you call them in advance and say "I'm working on a recovery program and would appreciate your help navigating the dynamics of our family". Chances are they'll be happy to help. If not, ask someone else.

Family dynamics can certainly be challenging (why do they keep bringing up my past? Why is my family so weird?). Dating in recovery is challenging (will they love me or leave me if I'm honest about my addictions?). Medical issues are challenging for anyone (what's wrong with my body? How sick am I? Will I survive this? What am I supposed to learn from this?). Transitions like a new job, a new house, a new partner, or a new child can be challenging for many people, whether in recovery or not. Births, bar and bat mitzvahs, weddings, and funerals can be challenging. The important thing to remember is that we have tools of the program, and plenty of good people who will help us navigate life.

> "In the book Hayim v'Hesed by the holy Rabbi Hayka (Hayim Heikel) of Amdur, of blessed memory, he writes: 'O man! Know that every day there will come to you some new test, either insults and abuse, or monetary loss, and you should see to it that you are prepared for everything before it happens, and then you will receive it with joy.'"[154]

Ultimately, **it is your responsibility to maintain your recovery, and to ask for help from your sponsor, coach and recovery friends when you need extra assistance.** They'll be happy to share with you what they do in tricky situations. Many recovery fellowships have phone meetings in advance of the holidays that help people navigate family dynamics. I suggest that if you're ever unsure of what to do, take some time to think about it deeply, ask God for help, go to a meeting, or call someone you trust. Giving service is a part of the program, so don't be shy in asking for help. It helps others work their recovery program, and odds are, they may have something wise to say. If you get advice from someone and you think it's terrible advice, then maybe they've just helped you get clarity on what you don't want to have happen. Often that's the best way to discover the way forward.

When I find myself getting triggered, I'll take time to breathe deeply, and think about why I'm getting triggered. Sometimes I can't figure out the reason on my own, so I'll talk to my wife, sponsor, coach, spiritual director, or a recovery friend. The serenity prayer often comes in handy, as do others from Jewish tradition. I always carry my recovery chip and a chip from the retreat center I was at with me. Even just taking them out and looking at them reminds me of how far I've come and connects me to feelings of recovery. Sometimes I'll use affirmations or mantras. Often, I'll sing a niggun, a wordless Jewish melody. Drinking tea usually helps and going to a meeting and sharing always helps. I also love looking down at my wedding ring, which reminds me always that I am loved.

What are the times and places when you get triggered? What can you do in those moments to give yourself some extra room to breathe and not respond from a challenged place? Who can you make a plan with ahead of time to navigate anything that comes your way? What affirmation can you say to yourself that will remind you of your inner strength to navigate challenges and maintain your sobriety? What melody or song inspires you? Write it down and carry the lyrics with you or download the song on your phone. You can always excuse yourself to use the restroom and play a few notes to bring you back to center.

It is tempting in our moments of being triggered, to slouch, to despair, to think about how bad things are, and to want to hide from the world (and ourselves). Tony Robbins says in those moments we need to change our state – stand up and stretch, go for a walk or a run around the block, do some jumping jacks and get the blood flowing again.[155] T. Harv Eker says "Don't believe a thought you think!"[156] Your mind will tell you you're a nobody (geez, you screwed up your recovery program again?) but you don't have to focus on that. So long as you're making progress, you're on the right path.

There will inevitably be challenges, roadblocks, and obstacles on your recovery path. I know you've got what it takes to meet those challenges and overcome the roadblocks and obstacles in your path.

"Rebbetzin Hinda Adler, the daughter of Rebbe Hayim Meir of Vishnitz, left behind her a trail of great deeds of self-sacrifice that elicit astonishment. Her amazing acts of tzedaka are engraved in the hearts of many who learned from her about the love of kindness…she encouraged others and spurred them on to support the needy, just as she did. She was so dedicated and devoted to collecting for charity and helping the poor that she could not truly understand why everyone did not act as she did. Once, an important woman told her that she needed money for a poor family but had no idea how to get it. The rebbetzin said

208

'Do what I do; walk around collecting money for this great mitzvah.' 'I can't do that, it's too difficult for me,' her friend replied. 'If it's difficult' said the rebbetzin, 'that's a sign that it's good.'"157

I know I'm on the right track when I set a goal that scares me a little. Then I have to grow myself to achieve what previously I thought was impossible. My blessing for you is that you keep growing to meet the challenges of recovery, knowing that the right people and teachers will come into your lives to support you along the way. When life is difficult – that's a sign that good learning is coming our way. May you be nourished by that learning and by your growth in recovery, each and every day!

Endnotes:

---

[1] Rabbi Evan Moffic, The Happiness Prayer: Ancient Jewish Wisdom for the Best Way to Live Today. (New York: Hachette Book Group, 2017), page 8.

[2] https://www.shatterproof.org/about-addiction/public-health-crisis-with-an-enormous-cost

[3] Melanie Baruch, Abraham Benarroch, and Gary E. Rockman. "Alcohol and Substance Abuse in the Jewish Community: A Pilot Study". Journal of Addiction, 2015. https://www.ncbi.nlm.nih.gov/pmc/articles/PMC4487707/

[4] Loewenthal K. M. Addiction: alcohol and substance abuse in Judaism. *Religions*. 2014;5(4):972–984, quoted in source iii.

[5] Ibid, source iii

[6] https://www.goodreads.com/quotes/23456-the-greatest-hazard-of-all-losing-one-s-self-can-occur

[7] https://www.asam.org/resources/definition-of-addiction

[8] https://www.merriam-webster.com/dictionary/addict#h1

[9] https://www.npr.org/sections/health-shots/2015/03/02/387007941/take-the-ace-quiz-and-learn-what-it-does-and-doesnt-mean

[10] adapted from S.L.A.A. preamble, in the pocket toolkit

[11] Charles Duhigg. The Power of Habit: Why we do what we do in life and business. (New York: Random House, 2012).

[12] Ibid and more information at https://charlesduhigg.com/how-habits-work/

[13] https://www.youtube.com/watch?v=ao8L-0nSYzg

[14] https://www.tonyrobbins.com/mind-meaning/do-you-need-to-feel-significant/

[15] Sanhedrin 70a:22

[16] Genesis 9:20-21

[17] Genesis 19

[18] https://www.vox.com/2018/4/24/17242720/alcohol-health-risks-facts

[19] Maimonides, Mishneh Torah, Human Dispositions 5:3

[20] Israel Meir (HaKohen) Kagan, "Chofetz Chaim" Be'ur Halacha 695

[21] Talmud Eruvin 64a

[22] Talmud Megillah 7b:8

[23] Rashbam on Pesachim 113a

[24] Rabbi Elliot Dorff, Marijuana and Judaism

[25] Igrot Moshe, Yoreh De'ah, Volume 35, Siman 35

[26] Maimonides, Mishneh Torah, Human Dispositions 4:15

[27] Arthur Kurzweil, "On the Road with Rabbi Steinsaltz"

[28] Menachot 42a

[29] Ketubot 62b

[30] Deuteronomy 4:15

[31] Hadar's Responsa Radio podcast "Can I Live Dangerously?" December 27, 2015

[32] Maimonides, Mishneh Torah, Human Dispositions 4:1

[33] Alan Morinis, Every Day, Holy Day: 365 Days of Teachings and Practices from the Jewish Tradition of Mussar. (Trumpeter, South Africa, 2010), page 106.

[34] Ibid, 108

[35] Ibid, page 107

[36] Pesachim 113b:2

[37] Pirkei Avot 2:5

[38] https://en.wikipedia.org/wiki/Emile_Coue

[39] Rabbi Nachman's Wisdom, p. 151, Sichos HaRan #48, quoted in Yitzhak Buxbaum, Jewish Spiritual Practices (Rowman and Littlefield, Maryland, 1990), p. 665-666

[40] Proverbs 3:6

[41] Alan Morinis. Everyday Holiness: The Jewish Spiritual Path of Mussar. (Trumpeter, Boston, 2007), pages 212–213.

[42] Adon Olam, traditional liturgy, translation from Shabbat Vayinafash siddur. (Congregation Bet Mishpachah, Washington, D.C., 2017), page 149.

[43] Rebbe Nachman of Breslov, Likkutei Moharon 1:282

[44] http://www.viacharacter.org/www/Character-Strengths#

[45] For example, https://www.mussarinstitute.org/Yashar/2015-07/middot.php

[46] http://rivertonmussar.org/route-of-mussar/middot-chart

[47] https://reformjudaism.org/study-48-middot

[48] http://www.aishdas.org/asp/lists-of-middos

[49] https://www.myjewishlearning.com/article/text-of-yom-kippur-viddui/ https://www.beliefnet.com/prayers/judaism/holidays/yom-kippur-confession-the-al-chet.aspx For a modern adaptation: https://www.atthewellproject.com/blog//lets-confess and https://opensiddur.org/wp-content/uploads/2014/10/Ahavnu-ViduiHaMashlimYK-Binyamin-Holtzman.pdf

[50] Pirkei Avot 2:10

[51] https://www.inc.com/benjamin-p-hardy/if-youre-too-busy-for-these-5-things-your-life-is-.html

[52] https://en.wikipedia.org/wiki/Simcha_Bunim_of_Peshischa - Contact Rabbi David Zaslow to order coins at rabbidavidzaslow.com.

[53] https://www.psychologytoday.com/us/blog/renaissance-

woman/201411/name-your-shame

[54] Toldoth Ya'akov Yosef, Parashat Va'yechi 39a, found in Estelle Frankel, Sacred Therapy: Jewish Spiritual Teachings on Emotional Healing and Inner Wholeness (Shambhala, Boulder, 2005), page 236.

[55] Proverbs 20:27

[56] Kli Yakar on Leviticus 6:9:2 - Yalkut, Sifsei Chachomim Chumash, Metsudah Publications, 2009

[57] Maimonides, Mishneh Torah, Repentance 2:9

[58] Ibid, Repentance 2:13

[59] source unknown

[60] Maimonides, Mishneh Torah, Repentance 2:2

[61] Ibid, Repentance 2:1

[62] Ibid, Repentance 7:2

[63] Duties of the Heart, Seventh Treatise on Repentance 9:16, trans. Rabbi Yosef Sebag

[64] Maimonides, Mishneh Torah, Repentance 2:14

[65] Ibid, Repentance 2:5

[66] Ibid, Repentance 2:4

[67] Me'or Einayim, Pekudei 1

[68] Maimonides, Mishneh Torah, Repentance 2:4

[69] Shmonah Kvatzim 2:97:1, Selected Paragraphs from Arfilei Tohar, trans. Yaacov Dovid Shulman

[70] https://www.quotes.net/quote/17139

[71] heard at live seminar

[72] Talmud Pesachim 66b

[73] https://opensiddur.org/prayers/solar-cycle/for-the-service/nighttime/bedtime-shema/prayer-of-forgiveness-from-the-bedtime-shema-translation-by-reb-zalman/

[74] Kitzur Shulchan Aruch, trans. Rabbi Avrohom Davis, Metsudah Pub., 1996

[75] Rabbi Abraham Joshua Heschel – see excerpts from The Insecurity of Freedom here: http://gatherthepeople.org/Downloads/HESCHEL_ON_RELIGION.pdf

[76] Abraham Joshua Heschel. I Asked for Wonder: A Spiritual Anthology, ed. Samuel Dresner. Crossroad Publishing, New York, 1983).

[77] Heschel. Moral Grandeur and Spiritual Audacity: Essays, ed. Susannah Heschel. (Farrar, Strauss, and Giroux, New York, 1997).

[78] Psalm 59:17-18

[79] Abraham Joshua Heschel. Moral Grandeur and Spiritual Audacity: Essays, ed. Susannah Heschel. (Farrar, Strauss, and Giroux, New York, 1997).

[80] Abraham Joshua Heschel. God in Search of Man: A Philosophy of Judaism. (Farrar, Strauss, and Giroux, New York, 1976).
[81] Overheard at an interfaith conference, though there is considerable debate as to whether St. Francis of Assisi actually said this.
[82] PSALM 69:14
[83] Mishnah, Pirkei Avot 2:8
[84] https://morganharpernichols.com/gallery/tell-the-story-of-the-mountain-you-climbed
[85] Soren Kierkegaard, found in November 15th reading of Answers in the Heart: Daily Meditations for Men and Women Recovering from Sex Addiction. (Hazelden, Center City, MN, 1989).
[86] Rabbi Jeremy Markiz's teacher found here: https://blogs.timesofisrael.com/pittsburgh-when-in-doubt-love-more/
[87] Alcoholics Anonymous: The Story of How Many Thousands of Men and Women Have Recovered From Alcoholism, 4th Edition. (AA World Services, New York, 2001), page 164.
[88] I heard this from Adam at a New Peaks/Success Resources seminar
[89] Overheard at an Enlightened Millionaire Institute seminar
[90] https://www.goodreads.com/quotes/3182651-if-you-argue-for-your-limitations-you-get-to-keep
[91] Maimonides, Mishnah Torah, Yad HaHazakah, trans. Simon Glazer, 1927
[92] Shnei Luchot Habrit, Torah Shebikhtav, Sefer Vayikra, Derekh Chayim, Kedoshim trans. Rabbi Eliyahu Munk
[93] heard at a professional speaker training
[94] https://mussarinstitute.org/Yashar/2017-11/mussar_lens.php
[95] Leviticus 19:2
[96] Maimonides, Mishneh Torah, Human Dispositions 4:15
[97] Avodat Hakodesh, Moreh b'Etzba, 3-123, as found in Buxbaum, Jewish Spiritual Practices page 654
[98] Authorship attributed to multiple sources. See here: https://quoteinvestigator.com/2013/12/17/breaths/
[99] https://www.campramahne.org/wp-content/uploads/2016/06/Abraham-Joshua-Heschel.pdf
[100] ibid
[101] http://www.gurteen.com/gurteen/gurteen.nsf/id/X00405372/
[102] traditional liturgy
[103] https://opensiddur.org/prayers/solar-cycle/for-the-service/daytime/birkhot-hashahar/asher-yatsar-interpretive-translation-by-zalman-schachter-shalomi/
[104] Vayikra Rabbah 34:3
[105] https://www.sefaria.org/sheets/114332?lang=bi

[106] Jay Michaelson, The Gate of Tears: Sadness and the Spiritual Path. (Ben Yehuda, Teaneck, NJ, 2015), page 119.

[107] Personal conversation at Author's Way retreat, November 2018.

[108] Rabbi Melvin Glazer, from his website and A GPS for Grief and Healing: 3 Powerful Steps to Help You Move From Mourning to Morning. (GriefOK, 2013), pages 2-3.

[109] https://www.myjewishlearning.com/article/words-of-comfort-for-mourners/

[110] Lama Surya Das, in Michaelson's Gate of Tears, page 1

[111] President Abraham Lincoln. https://quoteinvestigator.com/2012/10/20/happy-minds/

[112] Michaelson, 156

[113] scribd.com/document/73852

[114] Heart Warrior Chosa, in Answers in the Heart, November 13th reading

[115] https://en.wikiquote.org/wiki/Nachman_of_Breslov

[116] traditional liturgy

[117] Psalm 100:2

[118] Big Book of Alcoholics Anonymous, page 133

[119] Tikkun Middot draft curriculum, found online at https://images.shulcloud.com/428/uploads/PDFs/the-bechirah-point-rabbi-e-dessler.pdf

[120] http://www.greatthoughtstreasury.com/author/simcha-zissel-kelm-fully-rabbi-imcha-zissel-ziv-broida-aka-elder-kelm

[121] Proverbs 17:22

[122] Likutei Moharan 282:2

[123] https://www.drwaynedyer.com/blog/success-secrets/

[124] Psalm 96:1

[125] Kedushat Levi, Exodus, Beshalach 17, trans. Reb Eliyahu Munk

[126] Ta'anit 22a:7

[127] Likutei Moharan II, 24:1

[128] repeated regularly on the Every Day is Saturday podcast

[129] Deuteronomy 28:47

[130] Mishneh Torah – Shofar, Sukkah, and Lulav 8:15

[131] Mesilat Yesharim 19:101, trans. Rabbi Yosef Sebag

[132] Mishna, Pirkei Avot 3:12

[133] Sefer Hamidot, The Book of Character Contention, Part II, 13, trans. Simcha H.

[134] Psalm 118:24

[135] Poet and philosopher Asher Zvi Hirsch Ginsberg, also known as Ahad Ha'am. https://www.sefaria.org/sheets/90299?lang=en

[136] Rabbi Abraham Joshua Heschel, The Sabbath: Its Meaning for

Modern Man. https://www.myjewishlearning.com/article/shabbat-as-a-sanctuary-in-time/

[137] https://jewishweek.timesofisrael.com/for-many-orthodox-teens-half-shabbos-is-a-way-of-life/

[138] Genesis 2:18

[139] ibid

[140] https://tremendousleadership.com/pages/charlie

[141] https://mussarinstitute.org/what-is-mussar/

[142] heard at Millionaire Mind Intensive

[143] https://thriveglobal.com/stories/30-jim-rohn-life-changing-quotes/

[144] Ecclesiastes 4:9-10

[145] Rabbi Simcha Zissel Ziv, the Alter of Kelm quoted in With Heart in Mind: Mussar Teachings to Transform Your Life by Alan Morinis (Trumpeter, Boston, 2014), p.75.

[146] Heard at Success Resources America 2018 D.C. National Achievers Congress

[147] Answers in the Heart, October 29th entry

[148] heard at several personal growth conferences

[149] heard in therapy session

[150] Heard at Peak Potentials Conference

[151] Heard at Les Brown Speaker Training Program and in his audio programs.

[152] http://edison.rutgers.edu/newsletter9.html

[153] https://www.briantracy.com/blog/time-management/the-truth-about-frogs/

[154] Erech Apayim, 3:8, page 68, as quoted in Buxbaum, Jewish Spiritual Practices, page 656

[155] https://www.tonyrobbins.com/mind-meaning/how-to-reset-your-mind-and-mood/

[156] Heard at Millionaire Mind Intensive and at www.harveker.com

[157] Buxbaum, Jewish Tales of Holy Women. (Jossey-Bass, San Francisco, 2002), pages 46-49.

Acknowledgements

Writing this book has been the culmination of years of learning, in Jewish, recovery, coaching, and personal development circles. I want to thank those who've helped me grow, opened doors of wisdom, and helped me become who I am today. I would not be where I am were it not for the many people who have supported, challenged, and inspired me along the way.

Writing a book has been a dream of mine for many years. I'm incredibly grateful to Maddix Publishing for getting these words in print. Thanks to Matt Maddix for encouragement, and entrepreneurial wisdom, Denise Barringer for cover design (visit denisebarringer.com for all your graphic design needs), Sarah Ross for editing, and Noah Benoit for formatting, and Chasden Cole for website creation. My thanks to Angela Lauria and the team at The Author Incubator for showing me how to write a book and pulling it out of me. Special thanks to Cheyenne Giesecke, my editors Ora North and Bethany Davis, and the members of my learning cohort. Thanks to Rabbi Oren Steinitz and Denise Barringer for last-minute formatting wizardry.

Thanks also to all who've offered suggestions, feedback, and helped me launch the book. You have my immense gratitude.

Thanks to all of my teachers in the Jewish world, at the Solomon Schechter Day School of Raritan Valley, Camp Ramah in the Poconos, United Synagogue Youth, the Jewish Theological Seminary, Teva, Hazon, Storahtelling, Pardes, ALEPH: Alliance for Jewish Renewal, Ohalah, The Mussar Institute, Rabbis Without Borders, and the Washington Board of Rabbis. It's been an honor to learn from and with you. Special thanks to Danny Siegel for showing me the power of mitzvahs, Nigel Savage and Hazon for life-changing bike rides, and Maggid Yitzhak Buxbaum and Peninnah Schram for showing me the beauty and sacred healing power of stories. Thanks to Rabbis Ruth Gan Kagan, Shefa Gold, Mark Novak, and Andrew Hahn, and Daphna Rosenberg, Yoel Sykes, Jeremy Marais, Chana Rothman, Joey Weisenberg and the Columbia University Klezmer Band, Damn the Core, My Brothers Kippah Klezmer Band, and so many others for giving me space to grow musically. Thanks to Rabbis Hanna Tiferet-Siegel, Shaya Isenberg, and Ruth Gan Kagan for nourishing and shepherding my soul's learning. Thanks to my Teva cohorts for showing me what true love is, and thanks to Reb Zalman Schachter-Shalomi, of blessed memory, for the wellspring of learning you've created in ALEPH, for your friendship, and for the holy twinkles of learning in your Boulder home.

Thanks to Temple Beth El of North Bergen and Beth Sholom Synagogue of Memphis for giving me an opportunity to find my rabbinic voice, for showing me that I have what to teach, for learning with me what it means to keep the fires of Judaism burning today, and for loving me amidst the oys and the joys of life. Special thanks to Geo Poor for your selfless dedication and for being the best synagogue colleague I've ever been blessed to work with. Thanks to all the other communities where I've had the opportunity to teach. It's been an honor to learn with you.

My recovery journey has been shepherded by my sponsor, everyone who has shared at the meetings I've attended, and I've been nourished especially by the writings of Rabbis Mark Borovitz, Paul Steinberg, Kerry Olitzky, Shais Taub, Rami Shapiro and Dr. Abraham Twerski. I'm indebted to Harriet Rosetto and Rabbi Mark for creating and leading Beit T'Shuvah, and the Elaine Breslow Institute for welcoming me and showing me the magic of Beit T'Shuvah. Thanks to Sue and the team at Onsite and my fellow students in the Healing Trauma Program for allowing me to break open and showing me the path to healing. Beverly, Carol, and Sherrie, thanks for digging deep into my mind and giving me the blessings of healing and therapy. My thanks to Hope Presbyterian Church in Memphis for the many recovery meetings and learning opportunities. I am especially indebted to Reverend Pat Kendall for the gifts of friendship, kindness, and grace. Thanks to Aaron and Adam for our regular get-togethers. When are we doing lunch again?

I've been fortunate to study personal growth and development for many years. My thanks to T. Harv Eker, Robert Riopel, Adam Markel, Les Brown, Joel Roberts, Johnnie Cass, Mark Victor Hansen, Tony Robbins, Sam Crowley, and so many others for helping me set a bigger vision for myself. Thanks to Brigitta Hoeferle for challenging me to set and accomplish my goals and nourishing me in the process of stepping into the future yet unfolding. My thanks to the staff and students of Robbins-Madanes Training and Mark and Magali Peysha at the Center for Strategic Intervention for bringing out my inner coach and teaching me how to use coaching to unlock others' wellbeing. Special thanks to Taylor Tagg for friendship, forgiveness trainings, and support along the learning journey.

My thanks to the incredible members of the Memphis Advanced Toastmasters Club for giving me a supportive home to grow and develop my speaking skills. My Monday nights aren't the same without you! Thanks to the Washington, D.C. chapter of the National Speakers Association for showing me the path to professional speaking.

Special thanks to Sally Strackbein for mentoring me and showing me the way forward to telling and living better stories. My thanks also to my Speaker Academy cohort and deans for their wisdom and support.

Of course, none of my learning and growth would be possible without the love and support of my family and friends. Thanks especially to Joshua Gensler-Steinberg, Daniel Max Kestin, Monica Berger, Rabbi David Rahmiel Aladjem, Rabbi Laurie Green, and Chava Gal-Or for the gift of your friendship and love. Thanks to my hevrutas, Rabbis Heidi Hoover and Derek Rosenbaum for delicious learning and friendship.

Thanks to my parents, Donna Cilman Glazer and Rabbi Melvin J. Glazer, of blessed memories, for so many lessons and for the gift of your love. Your memories are a blessing, and it's an honor to continue your holy work. Thanks to Glazer surrogate parents Samantha and Jim St. John, Paula and Roy (of blessed memory) Klein, Arlene and Henry Opatut, Mark and Gale Dillman, and Jules and Judy Gutin for all your love and support. Thanks to Saba and Savta, Ellen Mossman-Glazer, Aunt Gail and Uncle Barry, Uncle Jerry and Aunt Debbie, Uncle Bob and Uncle Alan, and all the extended relatives and friends. Thanks to my siblings Avi and Debbie, Shoshi, and Rafi and Lauren for laughter, learning, card games, jokes, meals, and for the special, unique blend of Glazer sibling humor and life that only we can understand. Thanks also to Bobbie and Jack Vishner, Scott Vishner and Jessica Vishner for your support, kindness, encouragement, and love, and for adding even more fun to my family life.

Thanks to everyone who has helped me learn how to give and receive love, and most especially to my bride Sherri Alana Vishner Glazer, for inspiring me each and every day to fill our life together with love, joy, harmony, and song. Your love is sweeter than wine, and more precious than gold. I love you more than words can capture. Thank you for loving me, for holding me, and for being my favorite person on the journey of life. I can't wait to see where we go together. I love you.

My thanks to the Holy One of Blessing for the gift of life. I am grateful beyond measure.

To my students, readers, listeners to the Torah of Life podcast and members of Our Jewish Recovery community, thank you for welcoming me into your hearts and minds.

May we all be blessed with continued learning, good health, joy, music, connection, love, recovery, serenity, and peace, each and every day, now and forever.

About Rabbi Ilan:

Rabbi Ilan Glazer is on a mission to use the best of Jewish spirituality, recovery, music, coaching, and personal growth insights to help people live happier, healthier, and holier lives. He believes that suffering can be transformed into joy, we're stronger than we think, and everyone contains miracles within them waiting to be born. Rabbi Ilan is a freelance rabbi, speaker, recovery and transformation coach, host of the Torah of Life podcast and founder of Our Jewish Recovery.

Rabbi Ilan most loves empowering and inspiring people to embrace an uplifting vision for their lives and coaching them to set and reach their goals. He was certified as a Strategic Intervention coach by the Center for Strategic Intervention. Rabbi Ilan spent years studying the art and craft of public speaking, becoming a Distinguished Toastmaster, and was ordained as a Maggid, a Jewish inspirational storyteller by Maggid Yitzhak Buxbaum. Rabbi Ilan is a member of the National Speakers Association, and a Director-at-Large, of its Washington, D.C. chapter.

Rabbi Ilan received ordination as a Rabbi and Spiritual

Director by ALEPH: The Alliance for Jewish Renewal. He has a B.A. in Talmud and Rabbinics from the Jewish Theological Seminary and a B.A. in Comparative Literature from the City College of New York. He also studied at Pardes, with Nava Tehila, and completed trainings in the art of Sacred Hebrew Chant with Rabbi Shefa Gold, and in ritual theatre with Storahtelling. Rabbi Ilan was a Rabbis Without Borders fellow with CLAL: The National Jewish Center for Learning and Leadership.

Rabbi Ilan is an avid cyclist, and enjoys traveling, film, music, spending time in nature, appreciating every moment, and causing as much holy mischief as possible. Rabbi Ilan resides in Silver Spring, Maryland with his beloved wife Sherri, and their cat Taylor.

Praise for
Our Jewish Recovery
Coaching and Workshops:

Rabbi Ilan Glazer gave an engaging and meaningful presentation at Ohev Sholom. He is able to speak candidly about his own struggles with addiction and discuss it in an accessible and nonthreatening manner. He is a terrific resource for any community seeking a facilitator who can radiate openness and create a safe and comfortable space to learn and share.

- Maharat Ruth Balinsky Friedman
  Ohev Shalom, The National Synagogue, Washington, D.C.

I've always felt that the greatest gift that one human being can give another is inspiration. That's because inspiration gives you both direction and energy. Rabbi Ilan is a stunningly effective coach because he gives you a vision of what you could be. He's a perfect combination of encouraging you about where you are now, while giving you tips and techniques for getting to where you want to be. Time spent with him makes you believe you can reach your goals. He gives meaning to the word "inspiration."

- Mitzi Perdue
  Author of How to Make Your Family Business Last

This 61 year-old alcoholic, gay, married Jew-by-choice has discovered a weekly delight in my sessions with Rabbi Ilan. He listens patiently, responds with care, compassion, and considerable wisdom for such a young man.

- Jim N.

Rabbi Ilan is a steady, compassionate, and encouraging presence in my recovery process. His companionship is both practical and down-to-earth. I am grateful for his guidance in my life. Recovery is possible!

- Tom B.

224

Final Prayers

Master of the World, you have given us the blessings and challenges of life. Nourish us on our continued journeys of recovery. Help us grow closer to You, and help us live happy, joyous, and free, to the best of our abilities each day. Give us the strength to persevere through our challenges, and to find support along the way. Be with us when our hearts break open. Walk with us as we travel the road of healing. Help us find meaning and blessings each and every day we are alive. Holy One of Blessing, we ask You to hold us close, remind us that You are with us, that we are precious and loved, and that with Your help, we can stay clean and sober, happy, joyous, and free, one day at a time. May we do Your will, now and forever.

"Today, give us strength!

Today, bless us!

Today, help us to grow!

Today, seek us out for good!

Today, hear our plea!

Today, mercifully, accept our prayers!

Today, support us with Your righteousness!"[158]

"אֵלִי תֶּן־לִי אֶת־הַשַּׁלְוָה לְקַבֵּל אֶת־הַדְּבָרִים שֶׁאֵין בִּיכוֹלְתִּי לְשַׁנּוֹתָם
אוֹמֶץ לְשַׁנּוֹת אֶת־הַדְּבָרִים אֲשֶׁר בִּיכוֹלְתִּי וְאֶת הַתְּבוּנָה לְהַבְחִין בֵּין הַשְּׁנַיִים."

"God, Grant Me the Serenity
to Accept the Things I Can Not Change,
Courage to Change the Things I Can,
and the Wisdom to Know the Difference."[159]

---

[158] Traditional High Holiday liturgy
[159] Serenity Prayer - http://www.aahistory.com/prayer.html

226

Until We Meet Again

Thank you again for reading this book, and for making it to the very end. It's been an honor to be together on this journey. That you've made it this far in the book tells me that you're ready to commit to or continue on a life of recovery and healing. You're ready to let go of overwhelm, guilt, shame, and unsupportive patterns, and you're ready to step into a brighter future, one day and one step at a time.

The end of this book isn't the end of our time together, it's just the beginning! Please visit www.AndGodCreatedRecovery.com to download additional tools to help you on your recovery journey. I'll share with you the resources I use to fill my life with inspiration, learning, spiritual wellbeing, happiness, personal growth, and recovery from a Jewish lens. These resources are **my gift to you** for reading this book and for committing to show up bigger and better.

It's my honor to work with Jews seeking support on their recovery journey, and their loved ones. If you'd like additional assistance navigating the journey of recovery, you can **schedule a free call with me at my website**, or email me at rabbiilan@torahoflife.com,

I welcome your emails, feedback, questions, and any comments you have.

Please help me continue building a movement and community for Jews in recovery. You can hear stories and additional Jewish recovery wisdom on the Torah of Life podcast. **Subscribe today on iTunes or your favorite podcast platform.** Want to be a guest on the show or know someone who has a Jewish story to share? Please email me and let me know. Join the free Facebook group for continued conversations and community building around Judaism and recovery. **www.facebook.com/ourjewishrecovery.** I have a lot planned for the future of this movement, and I'd love to hear your thoughts as well. What resources would be helpful for you? How can we continue building a world where no one has to suffer alone?

Thank you again for reading And God Created Recovery. Until we meet again, please remember three things:

1) **Life begins when you show up and pay attention,**

2) **Today is a great day to have a great day, and**

3) **Now is the time to get started on your brighter future.**

I'm proud of how far you've already come and I'm excited to see you continue to grow in the days, weeks, months, and years ahead.

I'll see you again soon wherever our paths may meet.

With all my love and blessings,

Rabbi Ilan

www.AndGodCreatedRecovery.com

www.facebook.com/ourjewishrecovery

rabbiilan@torahoflife.com

Made in the USA
Middletown, DE
11 June 2019